Michael Angwin started playing cricket when he was 11 and has been a writer throughout his life. He has written mainly for his professional interests, which range from industrial relations to energy policy, in business, public service and public advocacy. He writes a regular opinion column for the *Australian Financial Review*. He has been playing veterans' cricket for his local club, Canterbury, for the past 15 years, recently for Victoria's over 60s teams and on three tours of England with Canterbury Veterans. With the encouragement of his teammates, he writes about his experiences. He is married to Kerry and has four children and four grandchildren.

For my wife, Kerry, and for my children, Kelly, Kate, Jack and Grace, who inspire me with their courage, resilience, ambition, humour and love.

Michael Angwin

Playing in the Twilight

Austin Macauley Publishers™
London • Cambridge • New York • Sharjah

All of the events in this memoir are true to the best of author's memory. The views expressed in this memoir are solely those of the author.

A CIP catalogue record for this title is available from the British Library.

ISBN 9781528997126 (Paperback)
ISBN 9781528997133 (ePub e-book)

www.austinmacauley.com

First Published (2021)
Austin Macauley Publishers Ltd
25 Canada Square
Canary Wharf
London
E14 5LQ

I would like to thank: my teammates at Canterbury Cricket Club for their friendship and love and for their feedback, support and encouragement; to the teams we played against for their goodwill and friendly competitiveness; to Francis Bourke for writing the foreword; to Bob Angley for the work he did to produce the cover photo; to the Wallace Collection for allowing me to reproduce *A dance to the music of time*; to the Yale Centre for British Art for facilitating my use of *Cricket on the Goodwin Sands;* and to Austin Macauley for giving me the opportunity to share the pleasures of veterans' cricket with a wider audience.

Foreword

I am delighted to be invited by Michael to write a foreword to *Playing in the Twilight*.

It is a uniquely diverse and highly amusing account of his experiences while playing cricket with Canterbury Cricket Club Vets since 2005.

I am blessed in that I and many others who originate from vastly different backgrounds and abilities have been able to play cricket together. It has been a privilege to experience such fun, humour and success as well as to benefit from Mike's ability to bring our experiences to such an amusing conclusion.

That our lives should intersect as 'born again' cricketers at Canterbury Vets is indeed a fluke given that apart from our mutual love of what some would call a game for eccentrics, especially given our vintage, we don't have very much in common.

Mike grew up in the western suburbs of Melbourne, I on a dairy farm in northern Victoria.

Mike pursued a career in public service, business, public policy advocacy and writing opinion pieces while I had ideas of becoming a farmer before having my 'road to Damascus' moment (fortunately) and coming to the big smoke to try my luck in Melbourne with only year 11 qualifications.

Yet here we are, some forty odd years later, it is my great fortune to say, that we have found ourselves together at Canterbury through the gift of loving all things cricket and of course, our club mates and their wives and families.

This book is not only about coping with such challenges as fielding cleanly a cricket ball coming at you quicker than ever before when you could swear that the ground under you has sunk at least a couple of centimetres lower than last season. Indeed, Mike refers to the numerous occasions when as a batter, he has been involved in so many runouts. Perhaps he found out the hard way like I did, that as you get older the twenty-two yards stretches to perhaps at least twenty-five!

Readers will notice that maybe on an initial appraisal that this book may appear to be about older cricketers playing cricket, more or less. But it is much more than that.

In the following pages, Mike's ability to reference many subjects cultural, gives the reader interesting and surprising insights into cricket, using facts and events which are completely unrelated to our game.

His brilliant writing skills and quirky humour somehow give him the ability to link the happenings of Canterbury Vets cricketers with historical and cultural matters, which is certainly unusual, to say the least.

To find ourselves part of a tale about such subjects as famous English painter JMW Turner, poet William Blake, the Enlightenment, Sisyphus and Greek mythology, Catholic doctrine and Papal infallibility, his broken finger, Tex's hat as a metaphor for ageing cricketers, Bugs Bunny, the Road Runner and Wile E Coyote, is exceedingly surprising. In fact, sometimes his style of writing is so subtle that I cannot be entirely certain that we are being complimented!

However, this collection of short stories provides a dignified and elegant account of much fun being enjoyed by many cricketers playing together. It provides a unique insight into grassroots sport at its best, being played within a community-based organisation with great people.

Fantastic effort Mike, and thanks for your effort in giving so many of us the opportunity to relive it all again. This book will make such entertaining reading for those who are not directly involved with Canterbury Cricket Club Vets too.

Francis Bourke

(Francis Bourke plays veterans' cricket at Canterbury. He has been club president and captain of club teams. Francis is best known for his outstanding talent as an Australian rules footballer. He played 300 games for the Richmond Football

Club of which he was both captain and coach. He played in five Richmond premiership teams and was selected as a member of the Australian Football League's Team of the Century.)

Introduction

One Friday evening in November 2005, I encountered Gary Gavin in the local Italian restaurant.

Gary and I had been cricket parents – our sons had played in the same Canterbury Cricket Club under 16s team – and, together, we managed and coached our sons' team one season.

Naturally, the restaurant conversation turned to cricket and Gary asked me if I'd like a game in CCC's Over 50s on the coming Sunday. He didn't need to offer me the tiramisu dessert before I said yes.

My cricket life has been average. I'd started as an 11-year old, playing Under 16s for Druids Cricket Club in the Sunshine Cricket Association. The highlight of my cricket career occurred during my first season when, as a substitute for my dad's team, I took a catch off his bowling.

My career peaked at 15 when I made 91 in a grand final, batting through the innings; and, in the next season, when I played in Footscray's Dowling Shield team, a representative team for rising young cricketers.

At 21, I stopped playing for decade, apart from a few games in England when I was living and working there. After returning from England, I played a season and half at my dad's cricket club and, more than a decade later, played a couple of seasons of Over 40s there.

I was nearly 53 when I put Canterbury's shirt on for the first time after another cricket-free decade. I've played every season since.

My veterans record is bipolar, characterised by many scores less than ten combined with scores at or near the veterans' mandatory retirement score of 40. My bowling, never a strength, has improved in the last couple of years but remains middling. I have had the privilege of captaining CCC's Over 50s and Over 60s teams, though I am easily not the best player. More Mike Brearly than Ricky Ponting.

My writing career is more even. I've been writing all my life in political and policy-rich environments: briefs, analyses and discussion papers; a couple of books; speeches for myself and others; advocacy pieces and arguments; journal, newspaper and magazine articles; and I write a regular opinion column on industrial relations for the *Australian Financial Review*.

I'm not quite sure how I came to write match reports other than that writing them is the duty of Canterbury veterans' captains. Neither am I sure how I came to the style that has been the basis of this book, though even my career writing can be unexpectedly quirky.

The reports are self-deprecating, gently mocking of my team mates, mostly an honest depiction of events which may or may not have occurred, sometimes thematic and, when so, often reflective of my reading of philosophy or with a made-to-order theme one of my team mates might have insisted upon.

Philosophy, science, the Olympics, dog shows, politics, business, the unique writing style of James Ellroy, Disney schmaltz, Machiavelli, JMW Turner, Greek mythology, Catholic doctrine, William Blake, *A dance to the music of time* and Scottish insular monasticism have been some of the sources to which I have turned for inspiration on a Sunday or Monday evening as I sat down to write a match report.

I am moved by whimsy and wistfulness, nostalgia and regret, gentle late-summer days, stoicism and resignation, languor, friendship and love – as the basis for an introduction, a sentence, a paragraph or a podium on which to position a remark about a team mate or a cricket moment.

I proclaim myself a reasoned and rational man but, I've noticed, my thoughts and my writing often drift into Romanticism and its reveries, of which I claim to be a critic.

By sheer chance, while reflecting on what I would write about a grand final we were once playing in, I hit upon a description of what veterans' cricket is like. I wrote this:

'During this time, I sat behind Tex and noticed, for the first time, the state of his hat which, I now realise, is a metaphor for Over 50s players everywhere.

Old, frayed, experienced, loved, not as effective as it once was, but serviceable enough to keep going without having to be replaced by a new version that might not see out even one summer'.

That's us, my team mates and our opponents, who are also our friends.

Tex is Peter Mirkovic, a former CCC first XI captain, veterans' player and superbly talented slow bowler who, sadly, passed away in 2018. I sometimes had to bear Tex's meanest stares when I terminated his bowling spell after less than the full veterans complement of six overs – and brought myself on.

Thank you to all my team mates for the kind things they have said about what I have said about them, for their encouragement and for their love. And for pretending not to know the meaning of what I've written.

Legends Triumph in Season Opener Over 50As, North Balwyn CC v CCC, Macleay Park, North Balwyn

25 October, 2009

Canterbury Legends began the season with a comfortable win over NBCC. It was an all-round victory: solid bowling marked by wickets in several unexpected styles, casual but mostly effective fielding and batting that lived up to its own hype.

We had good start. I lost the toss, saving myself from a difficult decision: should I bat or should I bowl? We bowled, at the invitation of NBCC.

First ball, first unexpected style. The left hander caught down the leg side off his glove trying to hook Goldy. No one's done that for forty years. Anyway, he was out. This dismissal was not free of controversy. There was some suggestion – made too late to be taken up seriously by anyone – that the ball could have breached the no ball rule by being over the batter's head. I consulted on this with the slips cordon after the first over and we agreed (1) that it wasn't over his head (2) that the rule allowed balls to shoulder height, which was the height the ball reached and (3) it was too late anyway. I duly informed the umpire, who accepted the decision with good grace.

Second over, first ball, another wicket and a lesson to all openers: don't cut early when Mirkovic is at point on bouncy wicket. Pete took a blinder and they were 2 for 1 and Ratts was strutting around like Dermot Brereton in his prime.

By the time Goldy finished his sixth and Ratts his fifth, they were 2 for 38, soon to be 3 for 44 when Tom Hickie took his second catch of the day off John Kent.

NBCC struggled for the next six or seven overs against Peter Mirkovic's tight bowling. Roger Bryce capped off a fine first over by unexpectedly bowling their number 5 with a craftily flighted – full toss stump to stump – sixth ball of his over.

NBCC's captain and his batting partner then proceeded to play some fine innings. Both got to 40 though we did let them off the hook with the Legends' enduring weakness: catching. Two catches were put down, including one by me. The next wicket fell at 159, when Big Pez produced the fourth unexpected bowling event, bowling the batter. With a run out in the final over, we had them 6 for 165. An honourable total, which would be a good get, if we were good and got it.

This was a little disappointing, nevertheless, given they were 4 for 64 after 19 overs but, hey, it was the start of the season. And, in an unexpected display of cricket inclusiveness and social engineering, we bowled 11 bowlers from the 14 players we had to choose from.

We then batted. This usually follows 'we bowled first'.

Gary Gavin gave us an entertaining beginning by being bowled at the end of the first over. Well, if you have to start the season with a duck, it may as well be then.

Craig Kent joined me at the wicket and was in sparkling touch. So, naturally, I ran him out, ignoring his call and forgetting the most basic cricket rule after 45 years.

Justice would not be denied, however, as I was bowled missing a slow, short ball that should have gone easily to the boundary. 3 for 30. It wasn't supposed to be like this.

So, it was up to John Kent and Goldy. Did they let us down? A resounding no! Both got 40s and we were well past 100 by the time Brian Clarke joined Dave Crothers at the crease. Dave was plugging away, a single here, a single there, another single here, another single there. You get the picture.

Brian began confidently but holed out on 8. Ratts came to the wicket at 4 for 126. We needed 40 off 14 overs. We had the overs. Did we have the men? Cometh the time, cometh the men.

Dave kept going. A single here. A single there. Was that a four? YEEESSS! And Ratts put the result beyond doubt with four fours. Both Dave and Ratts finished on 24 not out and we won with six overs to spare.

What did we learn? Our bowling is strong and we all think we will be nearly unplayable on turf. Our batting is adequate under pressure and Stygian only when necessary. It will continue to live up to the reputation we are inventing for it. Our fielding displays all the hallmarks of good game of chess.

In a fortnight we play Eley Park at home, 830am start. There will be no more social engineering with the bowling contingent. Misfields will be met with stony silence and a request to do push ups. Batting is expected to be Stygian only in a Greek tragedy. Captaincy errors will continue to be forgiven.

Legends in Second Triumph Over 50As, CCC v Eley Park, Canterbury Sports Ground

8 November, 2009

The apparently inexorable rise of Canterbury's Legends continued today. We spanked – I believe that's what they say these days – Eley Park with 16 overs to spare.

The victory was not without its controversies: what ground would we play on? Would it be turf? Would Eley Park turn up for a morning match? Was John Kent coming for a picnic or a cricket match? Did he care? And then, of course, there was the ticklish question of Rule 13A.

Today, we won the toss. What we did next would be a highly strategic decision with widespread ramifications. The match would hinge on those few moments as the opposing captain and I looked each other in the eye and I said, 'Mate, you can bat'.

In those few moments, I weighed up the weather, the wicket and the wind and decided to bowl, principally on the basis that someone needed to buy the sausages for the after-match BBQ and that would be hard to do if we were fielding second.

The pitch had a greenish tinge which the opening bowlers were to exploit with ruthless precision, their teeth bared, nostrils flaring, epithets flowing freely.

Early on, EP lost a wicket to the boyish combination of Goldstein & Crothers. Are they a firm of suburban accountants?

Again, the openers didn't learn. Slashing at a Goldstein ball carefully bowled to take advantage of the variable bounce, the opener was snapped up by Crothers – or Dave as we know him – just forward of point. I thought it was four. How wrong can you be.

Anyway, things didn't get better for EP. The first 12 overs was a period of considerable longueur, though far from Stygian. After Goldy and Ratts had finished, it was 1 for 21. And it wouldn't have been that but for a couple of lucky fours off the ever-smiling Mr Rattenbury. Goldy: 6 overs, 3 maidens, one of three. Take a bow.

The match took a more normal course after that. One batter got a forty but the bowling was well on top. Well, it was after a few uncomfortable moments for 'Tex' Mirkovic and John 'The Pic Nic Rug' Kent. The batters gave them a bit of stick though, as Tex was quick to show us during our innings, anybody can bat on artificial. The stick in the middle stages was 43 runs long off four overs.

Brian Clarke and Big Pez both bowled to their usual high standards. Clarkey was very tight and Pez was, well, Pez. The run rate slowed to a trickle and the wickets mounted up.

The fielding and catching were both superb. When was the last time all the batters were caught by team of Canterbury stalwarts aged more than fifty? Clearly, the threat of push ups has worked and I intend to use it again.

There were several stand out catching efforts: catches by GG and Roge deep in the outfield were inspiring (though I have to tell you that Gary said he only picked it up at the last second – having been previously distracted by the grandeur of his Movember facial hair – and Roge credited the 15,000 beers that explain his physique for the catch made perfectly by a combination of hand and midriff).

Macca fielded on the boundary for what must have seemed to him a lifetime. It certainly seemed like that to us. No, Macca, it's not that we don't love you, it's that your fielding is pretty good.

All out 132 after 20 overs.

Rule 13A. I knew you wouldn't forget. Can, and if so, when can a batter retired on 40 resume his innings? EP seemed certain it was just a matter of resuming the crease. GG knew better and he was prepared to look up the rule prove it. The consensus on the ground was that should let him bat because there were no runs in it. Whereupon I proceeded to bowl a no ball to the batter who couldn't score a run anyway. Fortunately, Tex snapped up the remaining batter at square, from which position John K has urged him to move moments earlier. Both Tex and the captain knew better.

We batted.

GG started his run feast in emphatic fashion: six off the quick over mid-wicket.

We lost a couple of cheap wickets (me – juggled catch at point, and Craig Kent, caught behind, Dave, bowled through a gap as wide as a Subway sandwich) but were being greatly assisted by the short boundaries. Tex joined GG and proceeded to play a most entertaining innings. Two sixes spanked over mid-off were the highlights in an innings full of them. I paid no attention to the critic who, with schadenfreude evident to all, pointed out that Tex's retirement at 40 put him only 12 ahead of his four bowled overs. Apparently, Tex wanted to demonstrate that anybody COULD make runs on artificial. You made the point. We know anybody can make runs on artificial. You just keep making them.

With Tex gone, attention turned to GG who, apparently, had not faced a ball for six overs. Was he asleep or once more captured by the beauty of his moustaches? That accounted for some early languorousness when he resumed concentration and the strike. But Gary tuned in quickly with another great six and several fours before he, in turn, retired.

Having captured the crowd's attention with GG's departure, Roge proceeded to play the innings of his lunchtime. Not even my appeals for him to leave the crease to give Macca a hit could deflect him. The crowd, with a roar that could have been heard in Balwyn Road, bayed for him to stay at the crease. Which he did and Big Pez didn't. Opening up an opportunity for JK who, rumour has it, fought off Macca for the right to hit the winning run, which he did with flair and precision, not to mention his bat, 'Old Faithless'.

What did we learn? Yes, anybody can make runs on artificial. Brian Clarke has still got it. GG loves to hit a six. We *can* catch. Both the bowling and the batting have width. The fielding has breadth. It's easier to beat a team of nine than one of eleven. John Kent could run a pretty good picnic.

Next match…uncertain. Scheduled for 23rd November but subject to a re-draw. If there's no one to play with, we'll talk amongst ourselves.

Cricket and the Meaning of Life Over 50As, East Doncaster v CCC, Zerbes Reserve, East Doncaster

6 December, 2009

Have you ever wondered whether the world is really the way you think it is?

Canterbury Legends had cause to reflect on that fundamental philosophical question midway through its match against East Doncaster last weekend.

Let me explain why.

Having won the toss, and being deeply influenced by Emmanuel Kant, I followed the Categorical Imperative to bat first; that is, to rationally follow the universal law that says you always bat first in a one-day game on turf.

I could have adopted Christian ethics and debated with myself what was the right thing or the wrong thing to do but Kant supplied a far easier answer to the universal question facing a toss-winning captain.

Early in the second over, the quick got one to bounce a bit outside off. Or had he? What was the precise relationship between what I thought I saw and what was actually in front of me? Could I be really sure that ball was out there? Perhaps I pondered those questions too long. The next moment supplied the answers. No, the precise relationship between bat and ball was not what I thought it to be. Yes, the ball really was out there. And so was I. A big nick to the keeper. I walked.

The brothers Kent were confronted with a different dilemma. They are the virtue theorists of the team, asking always 'how should I bat?' and answering, always: by cultivating the techniques, the virtues, that will help you flourish as a high order batsman.

Regrettably, Craig did this less well than John on this occasion, and so did not get his share of what Aristotle called *eudaimonia* – true happiness. Out for 6.

Next came Tex. This seems the right point at which to introduce the 'brain in a jar' thought experiment: am I simply a brain in a jar whose perceptions are being stimulated by an evil scientist? You would have thought so by the way Tex batted. No, it was actually the pitch. By this stage, it was pretty clear that not even an evil scientist could manipulate your brain to make it think the pitch was this slow. It was this slow and so was Tex, in getting his bat to the ball. Bowled.

3 for 15. The world we thought existed, where the Legends crush East Doncaster with the top 5 bats all getting 40, was clearly not the real world. Perhaps an evil scientist had stimulated my brain, which I was sure by this stage ought to be in jar.

Paul Grant joined John and opened his account with 6, 4, 2 in a row. Those three shots were the day's highlights and P&J continued in a courageous vein for a total partnership of 34.

Was this art? Frankly, as a spectator, I was responding to the partnership with a mixture of joy and aesthetic emotion brought about not so much by the quality of individual bat strokes as by the overall distinctive features of the interplay between the batsmen in their rivalry with their antagonists, the bowlers. This was a partnership of indefinable properties that more sensitive observers than I would immediately recognise as a work of art.

But Paul was still out.

And so was Clarkey, whose brief sojourn at the crease told us a lot about mind/body dualism; in particular, that is usually helpful to have them both in the same place at the same time. Unfortunately, Brian hadn't.

Mike Rattenbury came to the crease. His is an altogether more robust philosophy than most. Not for him the doubts of a Descartes. Not for him witty Socratic dialogues. Not for him a Humian inquiry into human understanding. No, he is more your *Thus Spake Zarathustra* kind of guy. And spake he did, 20 spakes, in fact. Still we were 6 for 96, and looking a bit vulnerable, especially after Deano's duck, 7 for 97.

Shortly after, JK retired. Or as Michel de Montaigne would have put it, withdrew from public life. Clearly, on a wicket like this, JK was the epitome of Nietzsche's Ubermenschen, superman, a follower of the Nietzschean approach to setbacks: never give in, believe in what you wish for.

Crothers, Burns and Bryce, basking in the Kentian sunshine, rounded off the innings and took us to 135, a moderate score with which Seneca would have been satisfied. Then again, as a Stoic, anything would have satisfied Seneca.

It took 10 overs for East Don to reach 20. Montaigne would have supplied them with a way of dealing with this inadequacy: that's the way it is; life's like that; every team gets to be 20 after 10 overs at some time and knows that, even at that early stage, a win is beyond reach. But he would also have said that it mattered that you kept going. And they did.

Unfortunately for the Donners, we ran two of them out in quick succession.

The match lasted another 20 overs with the bowlers always on top. Three wickets to Tex, 2 to Big Pez, one each to Clarke and Kent.

Karl Popper helps us here. The theory at tea was that we had performed poorly and that we were at risk. Popper's contribution to philosophy is falsificationism, that the aim of scientific inquiry is to prove a theory wrong. Clearly our bowlers proved the teatime theory wrong several times.

At tea, we did have cause to wonder whether the world really was as we thought. The final result restored, partly at least, our belief that we did exist in a real world, that there is no evil scientist stimulating our brains. We should take notice of Montaigne and not take too much for granted but ignore

Seneca and not be satisfied with what life throws up: that won't win us too many matches.

I could, of course, go on in this vein and quote Rawls, Gray and Grayling among more modern philosophers. Even St Thomas Aquinas could get a guernsey in a discussion about cricket. But I think I'll finish with Nietzsche, who anticipated the end-of-day at Canterbury Cricket Club:

'Last Sunday, I got drunk and I have no excuse, except that I did not know how much I could take, and I was rather excited in the afternoon'. Sound familiar?

(A subsequent note to me from *The Mail Man,* an ex-cop: "I reckon I might have enough information/evidence to go before a Magistrate and take out a drug warrant. Whatever you have been taking or using it certainly works.")

Legends in Shock Trading Loss Over 50As, United Eagles v CCC, Doncaster Recreation Reserve, East Doncaster

17 January, 2010

In a major correction to their rising stocks, Canterbury Legends Inc suffered the first fall in their share price following a sell-off by United Eagles NL on Sunday. In a day of market fluctuations, not only the Canterbury share price, but its whole business model was cast into doubt.

As the session opened, Canterbury's Managing Director released a statement informing the market of the company's decision to bat first.

Trading was slow to begin with and only got worse as the company's talented opening bat, Gary Gavin, unexpectedly departed the crease after a brief stint. Trading continued in a very subdued vein as the Legends adjusted to this shock loss.

Subdued but steady. The share price rose from a low 6 after the Gavin bombshell to a high point of 78, though the rise took an exceedingly lengthy re-working of the business plan by Angwin and Kent (Craig), taking 18 overs to add 72 points.

Financial whiz kid Kent was caught out after a well-compiled portfolio of 35.

MD Angwin shouldered the responsibility for the slow scoring rate and undertook to seek counselling for his own performance. As he departed following his temporary retirement, MD Angwin added that he was 'determined to see this through and I will have a better personal performance plan next time'.

The voluble but experienced John Kent was recruited to add depth to the sales department and went on something of scoring spree, accumulating 22 in a number of accomplished marketing manoeuvres before he, too, was forced to concede that he had tickled the till one time too many and left with a voluntary departure.

McKinsey rivals Goldstein & Galvin were subsequently engaged to stop the corporate rot, adding a combined total of 39, Goldstein departing while Galvin elected to remain with the company to the end.

Then the real shock of the trading day. United Eagles corporate raider, the very slow (medium-sized) O'Callaghan, launched a triple play on the Legends. In a greenmail rarely seen these days, O'Callaghan dismissed Goldstein, Mirkovic and Cooke with consecutive plays straight up and down the line, leaving the corporate stumps scattered in all directions and the strategic plan in disarray. It was particularly galling for Cooke who had joined the Legends only that day.

Thanks only to security executive Grant and the ever agile and nimble Galvin, the Legends recovered to post a closing final trade of 178, an unexpected result given the events of the day.

Attention then turned to the fiscal performance of the re-structured United Eagles. The restructuring had not extended to the opening bats, who presented a familiar brand to the opening bowlers. In fact, the brand leader, Bennie, had worked out a few technological quirks in his familiar batting pattern, playing much straighter than Canterbury was used to and pounding the bowling to all parts of the ground. Something to keep in mind for the corporate re-match expected later this year.

In an unexpected strategic misjudgement, Bennie's partner, Budgie, ran himself out, having misinterpreted the economic signals from both the strength of his on-drive and the market driven nature of the Canterbury fielding. Markets will always provide the incentive to maximise an opportunity, which Canterbury did; and Budgie was sacked.

Elbow had still not revealed his hand, sending others in before him and preferring to play a tactical game apparently intended to preserve the UE's strongest batting play until later in the trading day.

Meanwhile, the weakness of the Legends early batting performance was being exploited in the marketplace as UE's run rate, as measured by a far-from-ordinary index, exceeded Canterbury's by a ratio of 3:2. The ROI for UE was 6 compared to Canterbury's 4 and buyers were selling off Canterbury at an alarming rate.

In another of the day's business shocks, Gary Gavin showed he was indeed an all-round team player who could get with the program, run it up a flagpole to see if any one saluted it, could re-cast the vision, mission and values, re-shape the strategic plan and emphasise his task-oriented nature by both bowling UE's strategic and tactical powerhouse, Elbow, WITH A FULL TOSS, and taking a great catch in the outfield.

With UE's batting performance ratios declining, we were still in with a chance with 10 overs to go.

It was not to be. UE took 7 or so overs to acquire the remaining shares needed to complete the hostile takeover and position itself strategically for a final on territory that will suit its strengths.

Clearly, the Legends missed Hickie (accountant) and Clarke (CFO). And every business needs a bit of corporate muscle in the shape of a Rattenbury. Where were you, Rats?

The Legends should not despair. Remember the GFC? Share prices have bounced back and unemployment did not fall as much as expected. Corporate bonuses are still being paid and managing directors still have their jobs. I am particularly keen to have this latter point noted.

With some judicious re-engagement of key staff – see above – and a bit of re-work of the business model, we'll be in with a chance. The key business risk is the improved technology being employed by Bennie and the low risk of a second brand failure by Elbow. On the other hand, our own product performance in the bowling department is unlikely again to see 68 points drop from the opening pair's price in just 12 overs. We might rotate some additional staff through the opening 12 overs early in the next trading day if the Bennie technical improvements are sustained.

Conclusion: Underweight

Recommendation: BUY

Legends Win Again
Over 50As, CCC v Mont Albert, Canterbury Sports Ground

31 January, 2010
OK. No more philosophical meanderings. No more undergraduate humour making bad cricket jokes based on the finance industry…it's too easy a target anyway. What a bunch of bankers.

In any case, look what I've spawned in the 40s match reports. Laurie. Who calls himself Alexis de Tocqueville. There's a trivia question in there. Name the book by Peter Carey whose main character is based on Alexis. A lesson in sledging from John Kent is the first prize. The second prize is two lessons.

No, just a straightforward report on the cricket. You OK with that?

First, thanks to Canterbury Cricket Club for appointing the team's personal chef. Thanks, Jesse. What other team gets bacon and egg burgers fresh cooked? We look forward to the appointment of the team masseur and the style adviser. God knows, some of us could use one. Love that floppy hat, Macca.

Anyway, the cricket. It would be a 30 over match.

Rats didn't make it. Food poisoning, it was said. Yeah, sure.

I lost the toss but was surprised to find that we were asked to bat. Good. That's what I'd have done. The plan would be to score quickly today against the team last on the list.

Openers this week were Gavin and Hickie.

Hickie. For four matches he avoided the bat, unselfishly offering a spot to others. Now, he had nowhere to go. Tom, you're in.

And a good start. Tom hit three fours in his 13, including a great shot over mid-wicket. Complimented on his technique, Tom modestly blamed his golf swing but we knew better. It was a plan.

G-Squared continued his good form of this year with an entertaining 20 before he was bowled. I know you missed me, Gary, at the top of the order, but you were safe from a run out.

2 for 55 after 11 overs. Last match, we were 27 at the same stage. So, the boys were implementing the plan.

The next 14 overs went in a blur. Perhaps it was the Sunday morning but it could have been the quality of the batting. It was certainly a blur to me.

Three batters reach the maximum retiring score, 35. The Kents, J&C; and Goldstein, A. By the time of their retirements, the score had reached more than 150. That was more like it.

Have a look at the scorebook and you'll see that ideal over 50s combination of singles and fours…run a little and don't run at all. Perfect for old blokes.

The run fest (I've always wanted to write that) continued though the quality of the batting never reached the heights of the middle order.

Macca was promoted up the order. Like Hickie, he had his first bat for the season and clearly was a bit rusty. Equally clearly, Macca likes the ball to come onto him rather than to wait for it. He ran me out but I've forgiven him. That still leaves me several run outs ahead. Stockers' timing was very good against the slow bowling though he was out to a brave outfield catch.

Dave Crothers got a few and Deano just smacked them all over in characteristic style. Three fours. Big Pez was padded up expectantly but neither Deano nor Dave even thought of vacating the pitch.

206. Great score.

The Mont Albertians (thanks, Laurie, for your original contribution to cricket journalism) took an unconscionably long time to appear after the innings change. Eventually, they arrived at the crease to be greeted by a soon-to-be-injured Goldstein, A. Bowling shoulder. Lasted two overs. Thank God he can bat.

Clarkie opened at the other end and bowled a very tidy 5 overs for 24 and one wicket. I liked the variation. Rats, you'll have to impress me if you want that spot back.

Kent, J and Tex combined in a neat bowling partnership. John, 1 for 13 off 5. Tex was unplayable. He said so himself: 5 overs, 3 maidens, 1 for 7.

The match was probably over by the time Tex finished with them. At drinks, Mont Albert was 3 for 58.

The real star of the day was probably R Bryce. 2 for 14 of 4 overs. Bowling slow offies (is that what they are, Roge?) with the breeze, he had the batters bamboozled, enticing their high scorer out of the crease for a Hickie stumping. To be honest, though, even the Pakistani wicketkeeper would have got that one. Roge also extracted a big swing from another bat that gave up a catch to the captain.

Big Pez also bowled intelligently with no luck. 5 overs for 10 runs. Of course, he's only 3/4 the man he used to be.

The second 15 overs yielded 36 runs. 4 overs shared between G-Squared, Kent C, Deano and Macca added 13 to the Mont Albert total.

The fielding was outstanding and the placements are getting better.

So, there you have it. We won. They lost. The order of the world is restored.

Cricket and the Art of Politics Over 50As, CCC v Mitcham, Canterbury Sports Ground

7 February, 2010

Mr Speaker: The Prime Minister!

The Prime Minister: Thank you, Mr Speaker. I rise to inform this House of a matter of public importance, the remarkable events that gave rise to the Canterbury Legends' election win over Mitcham.

Now, as Honourable Members will know, the election was fought under extreme conditions, heat and flies and wind, the legacy of previous Governments' unwillingness to address the greatest moral challenge of our generation, climate change. It is of no credit to the electoral system that the Legends had to fight this election not only under the extreme conditions of climate change but outside their electorate. Yes, I repeat that, Mr Speaker. Outside the electorate! In North Balwyn, of all places.

The third disadvantage they faced was that they were placed second on the ballot paper, not by choice but by the serendipitous turn of a coin. So, Mr Speaker, they took to the field, steely-eyed and determined to let the Opposition know that they would seize and keep the high moral ground.

Honourable Members: Hear! Hear!

The Prime Minister: The Honourable Minister for Fast Bowling, Mr Rattenbury, opened the campaign and with wit and, where necessary, with a withering repartee, tore through the Opposition's economical batting. . The Opposition – and, indeed, the Government – was completely wrong-footed by the Minister's change of footwear mid-spell and voluntary retirement to the backbench for most of the remainder of the innings. But more of the Minister later.

He was ably assisted by his portfolio minister, Mr Clarke, the Minister for Opening The Bowling When Mr Goldstein Is Injured. Mr Clarke also routed the Opposition with a forensic analysis of their flawed batting strategy to the tune of 2 for 17.

The junior Ministers, Kent (On Field Tactics and Dissent) and Mirkovic (Aged Care, mostly his own) put the Opposition on the back foot for many overs with brilliant media skills.

The one unsavoury note in this for the Government, Mr Speaker, was the headstrong nature of the so-called Bowling Faction in our Party. Being to the left of common sense, they are sometimes ungovernable and need to be disciplined. I have not yet found the correct policies for this unwelcome task though batting any recalcitrant bowler at number 13 may well have a salutary effect.

(Honourable Members interjecting)

It is said that Minister Kent, a leader of the Faction, harbours leadership ambitions but he has personally pledged loyalty and, of course, a politician's word is his bond.

I should also draw the House's attention to the expenses scandal that marred Mr Bryce's bowling on this occasion. Mr Bryce is a rising backbencher with a good reputation, having acquitted himself with some greatly accurate bowling in his last appearance at the dispatch box. Regrettably, though with the same well-prepared brief, he was exposed by some talented Opposition to the tune of 29 runs from two overs. I have complete confidence in him. He was undone by the shift of the election to an artificial surface. We know that Mr Bryce has a deep affinity for nature and much prefers the green sward of hallowed turf at Canterbury.

There are moments, of course, Mr Speaker, when a Prime Minister must step in and show leadership. And I did on this occasion, Mr Speaker, and may say so with due modesty – for a Prime Minister – that three of the Opposition's front bench departed the crease, sadder but wiser men. On one occasion,

Mr Speaker, I was greatly assisted by my Parliamentary backstop, the Honourable Mr Hickie, who caught the Opposition out, literally, single-handedly.

May I also congratulate Mr Gavin, the Minister for The Utmost Seriousness In The Field, on the success of his new bowling policies, delivered slightly faster than his usual policies. And to greater effect.

Minister Rattenbury returned to the House late in the innings for another wicket and more repartee. Backbenchers Galvin and Macca also took advantage of the Opposition weaknesses to press their bowling claims for greater recognition.

With some superb work on the ground by the whole team and precisely placed fielders, we saw the Opposition depart, all Shadow Ministers dismissed, for 125 votes.

Mr Speaker, we took to the crease with Mr Goldstein, the Ministers for Knees and Shoulders and Chinese Massage, accompanying Mr Gavin. Unfortunately, Mr Goldstein received the most difficult question all day from the Opposition and was expelled from the House after only 10 runs.

That was the last of the bad polling news for the Legends. Mr Gavin went on to increase his percent of the vote to 40. His effort did not go unnoticed and, I understand, he is being considered for higher office.

Kent the Younger, Minister for Dark Glasses, was equally effective with 43% of the vote and has a fine parliamentary career ahead of him. He carried out many single-issue assignments and his calling at the crease was reminiscent of some of the best push polling seen in politics.

Kent the Elder carried his bat to 26 including two great speeches that drove straight through the Opposition's flawed rhetoric. And Mr Crothers, invited to the top half of the order for the first Parliamentary session in a long time, remained steadfast in defence and entertaining in attack as the voting drew to a close. One for 131.

We won the by-election and are now ready for the general elections to be held in several weeks.

Mr Speaker, we cannot be complacent. We cannot be satisfied. The challenges are great. The hurdles large. No non-core promises. No child in poverty. No working family worse off. We are ready, Mr Speaker.

Honourable Members: Hear! Hear! (Applauding, back slapping, three-cheering, for he's a jolly-good-fellowing…)

Legends Win Vancouver Gold Over 50As, CCC v East Doncaster, Canterbury Sports Ground

Semi-final, 21 February, 2010

Cricket can be like philosophy; or the finance industry; or politics; or like other near-life experiences, such as the Winter Olympics, which is the comparison made by Tex, who has taken to ordering up the themes for each week's match report. So, here goes. You can thank Tex for this.

We came top of the medal tally, 201 medals from only 5 events. Next came East Doncaster, 66 bronzes, all up. How did this happen?

We were first into the stadium. And our first gold was taken by Gary Gavin. (Your captain was eliminated in the early rounds.)

Now there are several comparisons for Gary's innings: it was the luge or the men's half pipe or, at least, the downhill. What a whirlwind. Wide sweeps to every part of the course; great leaps over the field; straight ahead when possible; got to the end of the runs – in fact, to the end of many runs – in the shortest possible time. A world record. 40.

Seeded three, Craig Kent has an avatar, the ski jumper. He knows only one way, straight ahead, backside up, head down. There is not a lot that's pretty about this. But he is very effective if can get some pace up early on. Got a bit of pace, but not as much as he usually goes after. Got some good distance. A solid rather than medal winning performance. 12.

Kent J and Goldstein provided aficionados with performances to savour. Kent, the distance skater. Goldstein, the ice dancer. Kent knew this rink, having ground out a workmanlike performance last time he was here. Did the same again. You can picture it. Huge thighs, modest speed, good at picking just the right time to make a move. Conservative like a good long-distance man is. Stayed the course for a long as he had to. Barely raised a sweat. 41.

Goldy, as they call him in the men's locker room, was a different proposition. The only comparison with Kent on Sunday was that they both skated on ice. Goldy was elegant, lithe, weightless, light on his toes, twirling his racing baton with unmitigated delight and enthusiasm. With twists and turns rarely seen, an ever-present smile, his performance was full of innovation. Presented with flowers afterwards, he could only blush. I guess it was the tight-fitting body suit that attracted most attention and many have asked him to do it again next week. Another 40.

After Gavin, Kent and Goldstein, I think we're talking ice hockey players. There is just no subtlety in some guys. Stockdale, Big Pez, Galvin, Rattenbury, Mirkovic. You would not want to meet them on darkly-lit ice rink. Think the movie *Slapshot.* Yep, that's right. Understated, intimidating violence. They carry on when injured, wearing their pain as a badge. Ya gotta love 'em. They plunder with puck. Set a target of 180, they got us to 201, scoring more than 50 off the last 8. What a bonus. Gold to them all.

East Doncaster entered, a flag bearer short of a squad. Rattenbury and Clarke, our champion biathletes, had their measure. The biathlon requires steady pace and the ability to slow the heart rate at just the right moment to fire off an accurate shot. This is comparatively easy for Rattenbury, who lacks any heart at all. Anyway, they surged in, ball after ball, and with slowed heart rate, fired their shots too accurately for the opposition. They only scored from three of Rattenbury's 36 shots and from only 6 of Clarke's. Both picked up medals. After 12, East Don were 4 for 23 and, effectively, this Olympics was drawing to an end.

And it was quickly put to death by Mirkovic. 1 for 6 off six in the Slalom (where his knees serve him so well).

The rest was a bit anti-climactic, like who cared after Shaun White had had his first half-pipe run. But let's record a couple of memorable performances: Bryce 2 for 15 in the pairs skating. Just picture Roge in tights. Macca's surprise medal in the curling. Yeah, true. His bowling is so slow that they swept the pitch as the ball made its way to the batter. Hickie was supreme in the snowball catching. And Goldy, back for another performance in slips, yep, slips, took three gold.

So, that performance gets us beyond mere Olympics. Next week it's the Legends Grand Final. Our second in a row. And many of us still bear scars from a defeat in the Forties by North Balwyn a couple of world championships ago.

Let's go Berries; or is that Snowberries?

Legends Win Grand Final: Captain's Diary Over 50As, CCC v Eley Park, Canterbury Sports Ground

Grand Final, 28 February, 2010
There is something about a summer afternoon late in the cricket season.

The heat has gone out of the weather. There may be a cool breeze. Some days, there may be a bit of cloud. Often, late in the day, it will seem to get hotter, as the sun gets lower in the sky and under the cloud. Of course, it can get hotter because that's when a match is at its warmest. An Alan McGillivray kind of a day. A Richie Benaud of an afternoon.

When there's a cricket final on, even the most suburban of suburban cricket grounds can attract more than the casual passer-by. That was the case on Grand Final day.

I arrived at the Canterbury Sports Ground, to give it its proper name, more than usually early. Nervous energy had the better of me. After all, this was to be a Grand Final.

But I wasn't the first. Tom Hickie and Big Pez were already there, hauling pitch covers, and those funny blue aggie pipe kinds of things that pass for a boundary condition these days. Tom and I marginally reset the cones that made up the eastern boundary. I thought that bringing the outriding cones five metres west would make a profound difference to the match. That's what nervous energy does to you.

As if to thumb its nose at the most thorough of John Kent's preparations in the face of ominous forecasts of much rain, it hadn't dropped a drop. The ground and the pitch were perfect, or as near perfect as a middle-class suburban council can make them.

Eley Park's captain was already there too. Clearly, captains of Grand Final teams have to leave their homes Very Early on The Day.

The team arrived in dribs and drabs. Teams always do. There's nothing anybody can do about it. That's the way it is with teams, unless you're on the team bus from the hotel. But over 50s Legends teams just have to come from homes, not hotels.

So, this was it. We tossed, using John Kent's lucky coin. Yeah. I lost the toss. We needn't have tossed. They wanted to bowl so they sent us in. We wanted to bat so we batted.

Clarkie was kind enough to give me a warm-up, commenting that my semi-final failure with the bat was due to a faulty warm-up which he could remedy. I felt more confident already.

Gary and I tossed to see who would face. He won.

Eley Park's opening bowlers were also kind; or loose, to be more precise. Gary and I took 12 off the first two overs, including a couple of fours that felt so good coming off the bat. In fact, we got to 30 off the first 8 overs. This was a good start. I could tell this partly because there was no Kentish sledging.

The crowd (yes, that's the proper word for it) had built up. Have you ever noticed how crowds 'build up'? They do not get larger. More people do not attend as the afternoon progresses. The size of a crowd does not get bigger. No, a crowd has its own special verb, 'build'.

Our crowd built up. It did not matter a bit that most of the crowd were Eley Park supporters. A crowd, to a Legends team, is a crowd. And a delight in which to play in front of.

Unfortunately, for Gary and me the special pleasure of delighting the crowd was not going to last much longer. Gary was bowled for 9, trying to repeat a shot that had brought him four in the previous over. And I followed him an over later, bowled for 22, playing over a slow yorker. It may not have been a yorker. I may just have missed it.

That brought the Kents together for 40 runs. It said something about both the bowling – tight – and the pitch – easy but slow – that the 40 runs took 12 overs. It's a long time since a pair of Kents took 12 overs to score forty runs.

Looking back, we might have known even at this point in the match that this would be a tougher game than we had had for some time.

Craig left, bowled for 17. To be honest, Craig, it looked like a bit of frustration had gotten the better of you. The 40 runs that your brothers took 12 overs to score must have been a rare event for the Kents and too much for the family to bear. So, Craig, we really do understand the frustration that occasioned you demise.

I looked at the scorebook this week because I wanted to know what had been the strengths of our team this season. One stood out. John Kent had been dismissed only once this season for less than 40; so it was really no surprise that he should make 43 retired in the Grand Final.

If I were fixated on reprising the financial theme of earlier reports, I might have added that if he were J Kent P/L and listed on the stock market, his price would have fallen because he had done no more than meet the expectations of the market.

So, perform to expectations of your best performances and receive no more than a passing reference of begrudging praise. That's the way of the world, John.

Unfortunately, Goldy soon followed, 7.

There was something about Goldy today. Not quite as crisp as usual; timing not quite as sure. I've often pondered this, usually concerning my own form: what is it about cricketers that makes them so changeable? Why do the skills that bring them a ton one week bring them a duck the next? Is it psychology? The weather? Biorhythms? It will remain a mystery and that means I'll probably never be a consistent batter. None of this explains Goldy's performance.

Anyway, to the ice hockey players: Stockers, Tex, Deano, Ratts, Tommy and Clarkie. For those of you to whom the descriptor 'ice hockey' is a mystery, please re-read last week's report. Last week, the ice hockey players got 60 between them, this week 47. The hitting was good though we slowed down at the end adding only five from the last three overs and getting all out in the 34th.

The crowd was still there and well and truly built and they were delighted, being Eley Park people. I think they thought 147 was gettable. We thought that we had the runs on the board and they were still chasing.

Teams always think like this. 'They're chasing' is a psychology of teams. It is an objectively true statement intended as a sober assessment of favourable odds, aimed at bolstering confidence. But it betrays an inner uncertainty, a silent assessment that things are in the balance, that the game is still in play.

A regular feature of our opening bowlers' 12 overs this season has been that those overs have yielded the batters not much more than 20 runs and yielded us a couple of wickets. There have been some memorable exceptions to this, as when the Eagles – mainly Bennie – took 73 off the first 12 and Goldy's six overs gave up 41 runs.

Anyway, this time without Goldy in the opening attack, the first 12 overs yielded only 29 runs and, more importantly, 2 wickets. Rats, as usual, kept the scoring low; and Clarkie, as usual, took the wickets.

Now, Michael is a sensitive man and I wouldn't want you to underestimate him. So, I have to add that the Rattenbury/Clarke partnership is highly symbiotic. They are a team. Rattenbury's ferocity and Clarke's guile. And the wickets belong to the team.

The next 12 overs left us in a more uncertain position. The unobserved uncertainty that we should have noticed when the Kents took 12 overs to score 40 runs was now very much evident. The game was truly in the balance.

Their three and their four both got thirties and had added 65 between them. The advantage we had after the first 12 overs had been whittled away. Advantages are always 'whittled away'. They have no choice.

At one point, Eley Park needed 65 from 78 balls with 8 wickets still left. We didn't know this. Had someone done the calculation and failed to mention it?

This period of play was highly unusual. Tex bowled tight. But Goldy, clearly not quite right, the Chinese massage in reality having been a few quick DencoRubs, with Kent J, gave up 31 runs from their combined six overs.

The other thing I noticed was how standard the fielding was. Interesting word, 'standard'. A bit like by the book without being exceptional. But I have been very impressed at how several of our fielders, Macca and Roger, have adopted very conventional fielding techniques that now enable them to stop the ball.

A captain starts to know more about pressure at this point. Was it just me, worried; or do captains always think like this? Do captains have a 'psychology', like teams? Who knows? I just know that captains have to make the decisions. It's no good asking for advice. The response to a request for advice is, in any case, likely to be 'Well, what are *you* going to do?' Fair call.

The call at that point was to slow down the pace of the ball, make the batters play shots.

Big Pez, G2. No one can slow down the pace of the ball like these guys, even though Gary claims to be bowling medium pace.

Then some things happened, as things can sometimes do. They have no choice but to happen.

Tex got an LB, which he modestly claims was a bit dodgy; and Big Pez – yes, Big Pez and G2 combined to run one of the batters out. Then Gary got another LB and Tommy and I ran another batter out. They had slumped – teams always slump, they do not just lose wickets, it's the psychology of teams – from 2 for 82 at the end of the 23rd to 6 for 89 at the end of the 26th.

But this match still wasn't over. Even though Eley Park lost its 7th wicket at 107.

While we didn't know it at the time, Kent C took a match winning catch. The ball being driven hard but uppishly to cover, Craig got good hands to it and it looked caught.

But we were being kidded. It popped out. In what seemed like a replay, the ball spooned – balls always 'spoon', it's the psychology of balls – over Craig's head and looked headed for the turf. Until Craig, performing a backflip of almost political incomprehensibility, threw himself to take a one-hander, while falling to the ground. It was poetry; or at least, really good prose.

The match wasn't over. One Eley Park batter knew exactly what had to be done. He had to hit our bowling out of the park. The next two overs gave up 16 runs and the gap was only 20 with two overs to go. Gettable, if that batter stayed in.

What to do? I bought myself on. Veterans rules require teams to bowl eight bowlers. Who would it be? I had hoped Tommy would be saying 'Roger' as he bailed me up when the ends changed. But no, he said 'You'. I took his advice.

Third ball, they ran for the second and would you believe it – Big Pez, yes Big Pez– hit the stumps with a direct hit from deep mid-on. 8 for 129. This was spooky.

Next ball, the batter who knew what to do hit me for 4. 133. Fifth ball, a short one heading down leg and I could see it going over the boundary. But no, he had swung too early and too low, got a top edge and Tommy, channelling Craig, also performed a backflip to take a one-hander. My last ball was a caught and bowled that seemed to happen in a dream.

Why was Goldy running madly on to the ground at this point? Had the DencoRub had an unrecognised side effect? No, we'd won.

Much hugging and handshaking followed. But no kissing. We wouldn't do that, even though many of us were mightily relieved at having won rather than lost a grand final. Personally, I was mightily relieved that Big Pez didn't kiss me.

The match was worthy of a grand final. Matches that 'are worthy of a grand final' are always called 'worthy'. Perhaps one day such matches will be called the less well-used 'epic' or maybe the bland ‘memorable’. My personal favourite would be ‘unparalleled’. But ‘worthy’ will do for this Grand Final.

Back-to-back anyone?

It Doesn't Get Any More Senior Than This Over 50As, North Balwyn v CCC, Macleay Park, North Balwyn

24 October, 2010
As I was saying, the over 50s good form continues.

The season opener – it actually felt like we'd just had a longer than usual break between games – took place last Sunday at North Balwyn. It began with a pitch inspection. Turf pitch, great condition. Surrounds, well, wet to say the least.

So, over to the artificial surface.

We lost the toss and were politely invited to bowl, which we proceeded to do. Absent Rats, we turned to Alan 'Mad Man' Goldstein, Canterbury's own Don Draper. Alan was in career best form, or so he said. What were you like as youngster then?

Well, it probably was career best. By the time Alan had finished his spell, North Balwyn was 4 for 25 and, even they would say, on the ropes. Alan had 4 for 11. Three bowled, one off a blinder of a catch by FW Bourke. You've still got it, Francis.

You don't see 4 for 11 too often in the 50s.

At the other end, Brian Clarke turned in his usual stingy performance, conceding just 12 runs from his 6 overs. His bowling is like a dark cloud over even the most optimistic of opening batters. They just get depressed and then they get out.

How he didn't get a wicket, no one knows. An enigma wrapped in a mystery.

The bowling stayed tight for the rest of the innings. John Kent – a more of a silver lining on a dark cloud bowler than Brian – and Tex bowled us through to drinks with the score still less than 50. After drinks, Big Pez replaced John. I lied when told him that it was for some variation. That's a captain's lie. I just wanted him fresh for batting. Is that a captain's lie too?

Tex bowled out for 19 off six, while Big Pez and Roger Bryce were both superb, allowing only 19 runs from their combined 8 overs.

Know the contemporary artists Gilbert and George? Big Pez and Roger are them as cricketers. Intentionally drab in their mode of dress, they take you by surprise with colour and movement. When you think you know their style, they change it.

The highlight from this period was the three run outs. From being our weakness, fielding has now become a strength, with the rest of us looking to Big Pez for inspiration.

Kent C and I completed the bowling attack. North, 7 for 107. Looked easy, huh. But some of us remembered when we needed 88 to beat North B in a grand final and couldn't get 'em. There's no room for hubris in cricket.

The bounce in the pitch attracted a lot of comment from the bowlers. And as there are compulsorily eight, that means most of the team, not counting wicket keepers (but who does that anyway; they're a bit like drummers).

There were various theories about the bounce. My personal favourite is that the artificial surface has a north/south camber and that the two pieces of the pitch had been incorrectly laid back to front – south/north – with the effect that the ball struck resistance from the strands pointing in the wrong direction, causing it to rise sharply. Some people actually believed that. But none of them was a batsman.

Gary Gavin sent me a postcard from Italy this week. While it looked like he wanted me to know he was having a good time, the real reason for the postcard seemed to be a pitch to keep his place in the batting order.

Well, he now has Dave Crothers to contend with. Dave opened with me and saw my back after I had flashed for the third time in a row at one outside off. Caught behind, 9. In an impressive performance, Dave stuck around until the score was 47, with an adventurous 14. Craig left one run later after a momentary lapse of reason which saw him bowled while apparently looking for God knows what in the heavens.

Alan G joined John K and we didn't lose another wicket as we eased our way to 111. This doesn't mean the next 10 or 12 overs lacked interest. Far from it.

John's batting can only be described as languorous, so relaxed was he as he stroked the ball effortlessly to several parts of the field. The van Gogh of the middle order. Twice, however, he was dropped. The equivalent of cutting off an ear and surviving. You have to watch that, John. 31 not out.

Alan, by his own claim, was middling them but then, disaster. The Knee Gave Way. Bits of bone apparently littered the pitch and the crack was heard in Belmore Road. The team was in tears. We can't stand pain. Retired hurt at 15 but hopefully not at 50. (Get it?)

Seriously, though, we do feel for Alan, who faces another arthroscopy. His comment? 'Not happy'. Don Draper, Alan's avatar, couldn't have put it better.

Tex, promoted in the order after Colin Peace and Tom Hickie declined a batting opportunity, put together a Romantic 15, all lush landscapes and booming clouds. It's hard to picture Tex as a Romantic, isn't it?

Big Pez certainly isn't. His comment on the victory? 'It's a long way to come to bowl five overs.' Where's your sense of joy and team, old boy?

Once again, Roger commandeered the score book and has made that pitch is own. Thanks, Roge.

Over 50s, one nil after one.

The Art of Cricket Over 50As, CCC v Eley Park, Hislop Park, North Balwyn

7 November, 2010

It has been said of Joseph Mallord William Turner (1775-1851), or Billy to his friends, that 'there is no more extraordinary instance of a great artist's evolution…Brought up within the confines of the neat topographical tradition of English watercolour, he left its limits far behind to soar into the realms of visual poetry and abstraction. By a kind of metamorphosis, he turned into a colourist whose magic conjured up images of sumptuous iridescence…'

Turner was also a cricket fan, having painted 'Cricket on the Goodwin Sands'. So, he actually invented beach cricket too.

I was reminded of this as I reflected on the victory of Canterbury's Legends over last year's other grand finalist, Eley Park, last Sunday.

Why was I reminded of Turner's evolution? Because I think there has been something of an evolution in the performance of the 50s. They have certainly left behind any 'neat … tradition'; or maybe they never had one. Perhaps they haven't quite soared into the realms of poetry and abstraction; but here are definitely signs of sumptuous iridescence. More of that later.

At Hislop Park, that *Archway with Trees,* we won the toss and decided to bat, fearing that if we bowled first, we would face a later *Evening of the Deluge.*

Gary Gavin, having returned from his Grand Tour of the actual sites of Turner masterpieces, was spectacular in the style of *Hannibal and his Army Crossing the Alps*, from which he clearly drew inspiration. A quick 17 got us off to a good start, as I plugged along. Craig Kent joined me at the crease.

Let's cut to the chase here. This is where the evolutionary story can be told. The middle order has gelled in to something approaching sumptuous; at least they batted as if there was a feast in progress. While only Rattenbury was iridescent, all got 30 or more. Rattenbury 38 (two sixers so towering they could have started *The Fall of an Avalanche)*, Mirkovic 35, Kent C 39, Angwin 40.

We must have appeared as details from *Sunrise with Sea Monsters*, so frightening was the spectacle.

No neat tradition here. All colour and movement, but not prissy water colour; instead, a vibrant, masculine, violent attack in oils.

But the time we were spent, the score had reached 188.

Uncharacteristically, John Kent played a more sedate role. Not sumptuousness on Sunday. More neat tradition. But again, I am reminded of an artist, but this time Rembrandt. He occasionally shocked his Amsterdam audience only to return soon and thrill them with his skill and imagination. I am expecting this of John (of whose innings Lynne, his wife, was heard to say, 'Not your most riveting, John').

The tail wagged like a study for a forthcoming major work, Watkinson, Galvin and Crothers taking us to 216, all Turner's apprentices in their application.

Then we bowled. This is where the evolution was particularly apparent. Short of the opening bowlers from the last match, we improvised, just as Turner had to as he roamed Covent Garden in London, sketch book in hand, plugging away, making his reputation, knowing he would move on and succeed, despite the odds.

Unlike his traditional batting effort, Kent J's bowling was reminiscent of Turner's *The Wreck of the Amphitrite.* There were no survivors, just screaming and crying, 'perfectly controlled and calculated to maximise the drama'. A case in point: John painted Craig at right angles to the batter and, next ball, the batter hit it straight to him. Out! And two more outs to John.

At the other end, Roger *(Death on a Pale Horse)* Bryce went about his business. Bowling droppers, balls that stopped suddenly in flight and had you stuck, so that Dave Crothers could stump the victim. Tom who? Roger also got three, including a C&B.

Deano and newbie Mark Watkinson completed the rout with a wicket each. Eley Park (could that have been a Turner title?) all out 138.

The other part of the evolution was the fielding. As captain, I no longer had to be *Ulysses Deriding Polyphemus*, on the case of the fielders the whole time. The fielding was great: 7 catches (none dropped), a run out and a stumping. What more could you ask for? Turner couldn't have painted that.

Canterbury Confidential Over 50As, United Eagles v CCC, Doncaster Recreation Reserve, East Doncaster

21 November, 2010

By guest match reporter, James Ellroy (author of *The Cold Six Thousand* and *Blood's a Rover)*

They sent them to Doncaster to stop the Eagles. They weren't sure they could do it.

CCC flew them in. They supplied first-class fare. They tapped their slush fund.

12:30 p.m.

They arrived. Mike got there first. Mike stretched his hammies. Mike bent his elbows.

He followed signs. People walked past him. They looked sucker-punched. He walked to the change rooms.

A thin man walked up. Elbow. He smoked a rollie. Mike said, 'What's wrong?'

Elbow smiled. 'You can bat.' Mike did.

1:00 p.m.

The ground was swank. The grass ran thick. Men snagged their boot heels.

Mike opened. Gary followed.

Elbow took aim. Elbow smiled. Knives in his quick balls. Brass knuckles in his slow ones. Change of tactics. Bennie and Strudel didn't get set.

Rookie – *cooool* Rookie – took aim too. Rolled up his hand. Made them swing low. No passion. Just cool, cold Rookie.

They were tight. They were slick. They had surprise. Surprise number two. Elbow only took two overs.

Gary scanned fielders. Gary got smart. Gary ran hard. Gary got out. 21.

Bennie took punishment. From Gary. From Craig.

Steady to 73. Mike got one in the leg. Blood, lots of it. Took him. Fast retreat.

Craig saw John Kent up close. His old bat. His old pads. His old repartee.

Craig played more punishment. He's a strong on on. He extorts singles. He works *gooood* sidelines. He pulls shakedowns. He gets 40.

John gets out. They watch him go. The repartee U-turns. Double-fold. And bad.

Rats was out. His head throbbed. The sun killed his eyes. Mike knew why. He missed it.

Tex dozed. He stirred. He heard something. His eyes opened. Light shot straight in. So did he.

There's Kiwi and Sars. They've got balls in hand. They've got form. They've got names on their backs.

Tex brushed by them. Brushed their balls all over. Kiwi gets even. Tex is mortal.

The end game. Bryce, Stockdale, Galvin, Macca. All over them. Runs everywhere. Its high stakes.

They tallied up. Nine out. 198 big ones. A cold 198.

3:30 p.m.

Bennie is back. He wants even. He wants runs. Bennie loves wet work.

It was overkill. And over quick. 32.

Elbow backs up. Elbow reminds Budgie of 'déjà vu'. Smiles. Runs the Budgie out.

It's him now. He's alone. Tex stalks. Tex talks quiet. Deadly and cruel. Works him. Tightens the pressure grip. Holds off the oxygen. 'I was letting him know that I won't go away'. Elbow goes away. Silenced by Johnny K, way out west.

Big H and Slurpie stayed late. They kicked Legends around. Legends got their rep. Said H did 31. Top-edged.

High up. Hickie took it. Smiled. Laughed. Slurpie took a hit. Left. Gone. Forgotten.

40 off 3. Eagles got headaches. They gnashed teeth. They chained smoked. They came home undone. They lost. 8 gone. 185 in the hole.

Mike drooled.

Absence Makes the Heart Grow Fonder

Over 50As, Mitcham v CCC, Walker Park, Mitcham

5 December, 2010

Half the team who played a fortnight ago went to Adelaide for the Test. Good luck to the Absentees! They got to see Australia get out on the first day on a near-perfect track (3 for 2, can you believe it!) and then got to see Kevin Bloody Pietersen score a double century. Who can stand all that self-confidence and alpha-maleness? Nobody. Well, except Michael Rattenbury, who would probably empathise with it. For him, Pietersen is less a spectacle than a role model.

So, boys, Australia lost and Canterbury Legends won. Take that.

We lost the toss and they put us in. Thanks very much.

Dave Crothers was promoted to the top of the order, as he usually is when G-Square is absent. He is a man of good eye and strong heart and showed it on Sunday when he scored a 'good eye' 22 in a first wicket partnership of 63 in 13 and a bit overs. At the other end, I sweated and panted to 43. God, it was hot.

Young Craig, to distinguish him from the Much Older John, put together a well-constructed 21 before being run out by (I've forgotten by whom but certainly by the middle order).

The middle order made a less well-constructed 11 between them (Older John and Long Tall Tex), both stumped off the off-spinner, eyes to the sky, clearly inspired by a Marcus North-like death wish. I was already hearing calls for their replacement by ...someone from New South Wales, which seems to have spare players ready for every grade. I'm told they have already been presented with their Canterbury caps.

(A side story: Tex asked the other side whether he was out. They said he was and he went. But he forgot to ask Dave as he passed. Dave, umpiring, had given him not out!)

Then, a revelation. Neil Warner, dad of Sam, played his first match for 25 years, replacing an Absentee. Neil clearly still has it. Run out in the end, limping of course, but with 16 under his belt. He lacked only elementary timing, which would surely return in a match or two.

Another revelation. Charlie Morris, an old mate of mine, hasn't played for 35 years. I've known him for 44 years but never knew he could play cricket so well. Scored only 3 not out but every one of them a gem. And no limping. More on Charlie in a moment.

And then there is Paul Grant. You can always count on Paul. And we did. For his 37 not out, which included some beautiful fours.

157. Hmmm. Not a lot for a team that scored nearly 200 against the Eagles.

We probably shouldn't have worried.

The first 12 overs yielded 31 runs and two wickets. John Allen was superb. 6 overs, 3 maidens, one for six. Brilliant. John the Older was highly serviceable in his first spell.

Roger Bryce was a bit more expensive than usual but I probably bowled him at the wrong end. With the wind is usually best for Roge. But he did get a wicket.

Then another revelation. Charlie Morris can bowl too! Well, I never. (Well, I did when I as young but that's another story). Three overs for 7, just when we needed to slow them down a bit. Charlie, you're a marvel.

We were very pleased to see Gary Gavin turn up to help with the fielding. On a hot day, it's just cruel to play with 11 men. So, Gary was a welcome sight.

Paul Grant's six overs gave them only 20 runs and Tex was again as stingy as Mr Scrooge (note the Christmas theme), giving them only 16 from his six. Tex has bowled superbly all season with no luck whatsoever.

I feel for bowlers sometimes. They toil, they think, they agonise. Catches are dropped. Stumpings are missed. LBs are not given. Fielders miss the ball at the last moment and it goes for 4. You can see the look of resignation and wear on their faces as they stare vacantly into the sun as yet another six overs pass, fruitless, wicketless, thankless. Bowlers are the faceless men of cricket.

And then, at the other end, a batsmen bowls, because someone has to make up the eight bowlers.

What happens? The batsman gets wickets. That happened on Sunday. Let's face it, I bowl complete rubbish most of the time. On Sunday, my rubbish was so bad, the garbage guys wouldn't have touched it. But three batsmen did, for three catches, by Tex, Dave and Charlie (you can't keep me out of the game) Morris. Sorry bowlers.

Gary Gavin, Craig the Younger and John the Older completed the innings and, notwithstanding a few moments when our collective heart rate rose, we won with 16 runs to spare.

Speaking of spare, spare a thought for John Stan, up from the 40s, knows no one in the 50s, to help out. He was a terrier. All over the place in the field, a smile for everyone. Saved us a bucketload. He thanked me after the game for letting him play. I repaid his kindness by giving him neither a bat nor a bowl. That's cricket, John. See me next match.

BTW, the next match is on 16 January. Middle of the summer holiday season. So, I'm getting in now. Who's up for it on 16 January? I'd like to try and settle this before Christmas. Get those YESs coming in.

Just Remember, Rats, You Asked for it
Over 50As, CCC v Mont Albert, Canterbury Sports Ground

16 January, 2011

Cricket, like any form of life, has its characters. We classify those characters in a variety of ways: heroes and villains; the good, the bad and the ugly; or, in the case of Rats' request for this match report, superheroes and cartoon characters.

Let the fun begin. Canterbury v Mont Albert at Hislop Park, last Sunday.

As captain, I feel I ought to be able to give myself a respectable avatar and my first choice would be Brains, from Thunderbirds.

But for reasons that will become apparent in this match, Wile E Coyote is probably more apt.

Like Wile E, I gained a temporary personal disadvantage by losing the toss and being asked to bowl.

We opened with the usual combination of Batman and Robin, better known as Rats and Clarkie. 12 overs of morally enviable bowling, selfless, altruistic and professional. Doesn't sound like Rats, does it?

Only 32 runs scored from them. What more can you ask of these guys? A wicket would have been a bonus. But let's not be too critical of the Scraped Crusader and his erstwhile sidekick. They set up the match for us again.

Next up was Bugs Bunny. Who else would John Kent be? That wascally wabbit; that wise quacking wiseacre. Four overs, one for seven. Have a carrot, John.

Joined at the other end by Tex. Tex doesn't need an avatar, a character. He's already one in himself. People choose Tex as their character. Several other Canterbury bowlers have asked me if they could be Tex. I've told them Tex's character is not mine to give away. But if they adopted the right persona of superior talent combined with a moral high ground of deserved success unjustly denied, then they could be Tex too. Five overs for 15, no wickets.

First four superheroes. 21 overs for 54 runs between them. We were well on the way. What did it matter that there was only one wicket at this point. Though it is worth noting that Inspector Gadget Gavin, with long arms stretched to the limit took the catch that gave us the wicket off Bugs' bowling.

The next 15 overs yielded 63 runs from a variety of superhuman efforts by Mark (the Green Hornet) Watkinson and Roger (The Joker) Bryce.

Dean Galvin (Superboy) actually took a wicket on a largely lifeless pitch.

Alan Goldstein, the Invisible Man, made a strange return to the crease, bowling three overs at the death. That scared everybody, not least the batters.

Mont Albert made 117. Gettable.

Why Wile E Coyote? Because all my plans came to nothing and I kept falling over injured.

The pattern repeated itself with my batting. The plan was to pummel the bowling lifeless and be the day's superhero with a quickfire 40.

Of course, that didn't work out. Top edge to the second ball and I went the way of Wile E, outsmarted again by a scrawny road runner of a bowler. I spent the rest of the day sulking.

Now, who reckons Dave Crothers looks like Lex Luther? Well, he does. Nothing to do with his batting and nothing to do with the story. Dave made three but enjoyed himself in that evil Lex Luther kind of way. I guess he might have felt like he should imprison a bowler or two in an ice cell in the Arctic. But Dave is too nice ever to be Lex. Stay as sweet as you are, Dave.

The departure of Wile E and Lex paved the way for two true superheroes: Kent, now incarnated as Indiana Jones, swashbuckling and wisecracking his way across the game; and Gary Gavin, now being John McCain from *Die Hard*, taking risk after risk to save us from ourselves. Both got forties. Wrapped up the game. Left room for the comedy that was to follow.

Enter Goldy, not quite as invisible as before, with a respectable 11 not out.

Enter Rats. Now this is where it gets interesting. You know those kinds of bowlers who pitch them above the eyeline and they bounce and you don't quite know what to do with them. You can use your feet to get them on the full but that's pretty risky for old blokes. Or you can try and bunt them to the ground but you can never get more than two or three runs an over.

Or you can innovate. Like by trying to swat the ball over the keeper's head or you turn to your wrong hand to belt them in the opposite direction. Good players can do that. Others just fall over. Rats, Mr Magoo, you've done it again. But you did make 7. To round things out, Tex got 8 and we won with 10 overs to spare.

An expected victory albeit one where we took few wickets and the fielding was ordinary. Superheroes we are definitely not. Christmas cobwebs are gone and there are no excuses left.

The only thing left to do was watch the exciting end to the other Vets match.

The New Romantics
Over 50As, CCC v Eley Park, Canterbury Sports Ground

20 February, 2011

Since the eighteenth century, there has been a constant struggle, in philosophy and art, in literature and life, between the logic and cool reason of the Enlightenment and the exquisite introspection and pain of Romanticism.

Those of you who know me well will testify that I am horrified by Romanticism. I hold it responsible for most of the disasters of the last 100 years including the Second World War, the Sixties, flares and body shirts, Duran Duran, graffiti and Senator Bob Brown.

In fact, Romanticism is probably the cause of the looming disintegration of the West and, unless we do something about, we'll all have to wear body shirts again, this time compulsorily. How would that look on a bunch of over 50s cricketers?

You see what kind of trouble we are in?

That's why I am quite confused. Because yesterday's semi-final victory by the Canterbury Legends over Eley Park was not achieved by logic and cool reason; but by the imagination and passion of haemorrhaging Romanticism.

How is a logical, reasoned child of the Enlightenment meant to cope with that? What does one do when one's world view is so amply demonstrated to have failed? And when the alternative world view has triumphed so comprehensively?

Romantics would say, go with the flow.

What am I to do?

In my world, the Enlightenment First XI would be captained by Steve Waugh with Greg Chappell and David Gowers as its leading batsmen. All straight lines and cool strokes. The bowling would be led by Michael Holding and Imran Khan, all perfectly balanced run-up and inexorable, logical success.

The Romantic First XI would be captained by Rick Darling; and Graeme Hick and VVS Laxman, both tragic figures, would be the first batters selected. Steve Harmison would open the bowling and Harbhajan Singh would bowl spin.

See what I mean?

The victory I imagined for yesterday had me winning the toss, Gary Gavin and I making a 50 opening partnership, the next three batters each getting 40 and the tail wagging with 50 off the last six overs. 220. Easy logic.

Then Goldy, Clarkie, Rats and Tex would bowl 24 overs of tight reason with Eley Park 4 for 90; and wisely calculating their slim hopes. Roger and Deano would lead the attack for the last 12 overs while I made sure everybody got a chance to contribute as the Parkers folded for 134.

Did that happen? No. Instead, we go through exquisite Romantic pain, with thundering lows and booming highs. We are not cool. We throw out logic. We suffer extreme emotion. There is even a Romantic hero.

I lost the toss and, I can't believe this, they put us in.

But my first disillusioning experience is coming quickly.

We are 3 for 14. I'm out again, slashing outside the off. Gary goes for a duck, walking, off a dropped catch; and Kent J, all straight lines and cool strokes, is out for 2.

We struggle. At drinks we have recovered a bit, thanks to Kent C and Goldy, who get us to 3 for 64. But a worse Romantic twist is about to occur. At 69, Goldy goes for 28 , at 71 Craig follows for 29 and then Rats is out for 1. We are 6 for 71 and all but overcome by the weariness of life, overawed by the Wordsworthian passion of Eley Park's bowlers.

But Romantic literature has more twists than a soap opera scandal. And more twists were to come.

By now, we had those two Ancient Mariners at the crease. (Get the Samuel Taylor Coleridge reference?) Tex and Paul Grant. They are magnificent in their noble savage kind of way. They take us to 129 before Tex is out stumped for 28. But they have restored symmetry to the game. Symmetry is, of course, logical and almost never found in Romantic allusion, which thrives on asymmetry, which is how the game has unfolded until now.

The last four overs give us another 19 runs, as Paul continues his plunder (great Romantic word) for 39 not out with contributions from Clarkie and Dave Cothers. We finish on 148, spookily similar to last year's grand final score of 147.

With a measure of Enlightenment values returned to the game, we come out after tea more confident.

Twenty-one overs later they are none for 79 with one batter retired. We suffer a severe depression, as if contemplating the demise of an ancient tree in a poem by William Blake.

It wasn't that the bowlers had not bowled well. In fact, my estimation of Eley Park's drinks score was between 60 and 70 and they were, in fact, 64 at drinks.

But it didn't feel right and we were under pressure with 9 wickets to fall and only 70 runs to beat us off 14 overs.

I think Tex was a bit gobsmacked when I replaced him with Mark Watkinson after only two overs. But, by now, I'd thrown out logic and was no longer cool and, to quote Laurie Cavill, I gotta tell you, captaincy is not all beer and skittles, you know. How Romantic is that?

We had to try something different and so Mark and Roger Bryce bowled four respectable over between them.

Then we brought Paul Grant on, bowling his darts from one end, and John Kent came on at the other end.

Paul got a wicket in his first over, finally getting Crowie out caught. John's tactic was to speed up the pace of the game as we spread the field. This gave us a bit more control over events.

Overs 22 to 29 were any Romantic's dream, as we overcame adversity with imagination and passion. Reason and logic had nothing to do with it. Cool heads had become fevered brows.

Eley Park went from 1 for 79 to 6 for 95 in those 8 overs. Dramatic catches were taken as if they were child's play which, in Romantic imagination, they are. Gary Gavin and Mark W both took great catches.

Ziggy was strangely subdued at the crease, as if overcome by some magic emanating from the bowlers' hands. You can say magic when being a Romantic. Notwithstanding 11 from each of Ziggy and Greeny and 8 from The Hawk, we had them gone for 123. (I was hoping for 134 but 123 is good enough).

And we did have a genuine hero, in the best of Romantic tradition. Our Mr Darcy. Our towering alpine peak. Our shimmering lake. Paul Grant got 5 for 13 off 6 overs, the best performance I've seen with the ball in vets. And John's 1 for 20 but more importantly, his tactical sense, his logic and reason, helped us through. As if not to be outdone, Rats got the last two wickets, both bowled.

Phew.

So, we beat Eley Park again in a Titanic contest. They are a good side and we will have more close contests.

But next Sunday, the old foe, United Eagles. I'd like to think that logic and reason will prevail next week and we will win in the way I shape the game in my dreams. But I wouldn't bet on it. So, there will be no plan for next week. We'll just go with the Romantic flow.

Let me know if you are an 'in' next week. And invite your families and friends to CSG. We still need lots of logic and reason on the side-lines.

Turn Off the Lights, Stop the Clocks Over 50As, CCC v United Eagles, Canterbury Sports Ground

Grand Final, 27 February, 2011
There is no easy way around this. No clever allegories or Romantic allusions can hide the truth. Let's make it short and sweet, not least because I am reduced to one finger typing today.

We lost. They won.

Comprehensively.

Can't blame the weather, though it played a part in the game.

We won the toss and batted at a somewhat soggy Canterbury. We lost five early wickets and were in real trouble at 5 for 34.

Thanks to Gary Gavin, Tex and The Mailman, who all batted very well for 20s and 30s, we got to 132, which I thought was a par score in the conditions. With the Eagles at 3 for 51, we were in with a chance. Elbow and Bennie were out and the bowlers were doing well.

It didn't last, I'm told, having departed for hospital with a broken finger.

Apparently, they went the tonk, probably wise in the conditions, and got the runs with 8 overs to spare.

Well, that's it. Season over.

But it was still a good season. Lots of old blokes got to do something they love and we had a lot of success. Good team spirit and much good humour.

The Rites of Spring

20 August, 2011
A note to my cricketing colleagues.

I got out of bed this morning to go and get the coffee as I usually do on a Saturday morning. The fog was lifting and the sun was beginning to shine through. When I got back with the coffee, I noticed that the rose bushes I had pruned last weekend had sprouted. The Manchurian pears were in blossom and the cherry plum was littering the lawn with white flowers. I could smell the pittosporum.

This, of course, is a prelude.

Last evening, I ran into Laurie Cavill at the local wine shop. Now, this may surprise you, but Laurie is a different man in a tie. He looked very lawyerly and, I have to stay, I was pretty impressed, not the least with the quality of the wine lawyers can apparently afford to buy.

Laurie and I got talking. Naturally, we talked about cricket. The progress of the Australians, how good the English are, thank God Hilditch is on the way out. Normal kind of chatter. Out of the blue, Laurie suggested an indoor net, sometime next week.

Now, some of you may think this is a trifle enthusiastic. Rattenbury and Mirkovic will be guffawing. But I've decided to let Laurie have his head on this.

So, back to spring. The annual Maddox brochure arrived in the mail yesterday; so, I know it is spring and that the cricket season is upon us. 7 to 8 weeks away by my calculation. Not too early for a net. So, for those of you with flexible calves and stretched hammies and arms that can still be lifted above your shoulders and keen on sharpening your reflexes, reply to me and Laurie and Laurie will take it from there.

The Canterbury Legends Played the United Eagles on Sunday and Won Over 50As, CCC v United Eagles, Canterbury Sports Ground

6 November, 2011
Sunday was one of those days that just wouldn't make up its mind what kind of day it wanted to be. Did it want to be hot? Did it want to rain? Who knows. Sometimes, Sundays can be like that. Indecisive.

I didn't trust last Sunday. So, I took two hats and my jumper. Just on case.

Th Eagles beat us in last year's grand final so this was what the AFL would call a rematch or, if their marketing people really were at a loss, a blockbuster. So, we'll call it a blockbuster.

When you play the Eagles, you don't toss. You have a welcoming chat with the captain ('G'day Elbow. G'day Mike'). And then you say, 'Do you want to bowl?' Cause you know they do. And you want to bat. So, you do.

We opened with Gary Gavin and Michael Kent. They did well. It was pretty clear that Gary was tiring early and he went the tonk. A not unusual tactic for a tiring opener on what was still a warm day. And quite a tonk it was.

By the time he tonked out at 34, we were 50 and feeling pretty smug, I can tell you.

Smug is usually a mistake. Like its cousin, hubris, smugness is often the precursor to a fall. As it was with the middle order. Now, I draw no conclusion from this – and I say this with no schadenfreude whatsoever – but the middle order comprised Kent, Kent and Kent. Well, Mike is an opener. But that doesn't fit my story so he can be middle order for its purposes. Three quick wickets. Mike had accumulated a few. Which is just as well because his brothers got exactly none between them. I repeat. No schadenfreude.

I didn't see Craig go out (so I can't write a clever description of it) but I know John was run out at the bowler's end, having faced just one ball. Nought. Nil. Zip. Zilch. Then Mike was out as well.

SUDDENLY, we were 4 for 52 and hubris had become humble. We now had a lot to be humble about.

I joined Tex who was in sparkling (sparkling is always the adjective used to describe entertaining batting) form. And we reached 70-odd before I got a leading edge to end my ragged innings. 5 down. At this stage (after I had thrown my equipment around the dressing room in the only way I could emulate Ricky Ponting), we were saying that 130 would still be competitive. And the warm and mellow feeling we had at none for 40 had become dyspeptic.

Worry? What, me worry?

You bet. I really wanted to win this match and it was just not unfolding in the way I had carefully constructed in my mind.

But I needn't have worried so much. Tex got his 40. Followed in quick order by Bob Angley and Paul Grant. What a luxury it is to have those guys batting at 7 and 8. Sitting with David Hastings, we were speculating about the eventual score. I was settling for 150 but Dave was pushing it up. First to 170, them to 200, then to 220. I was sceptical but I let him go unchallenged, as you do with the new addition to the team. But David clearly knows his cricket. After the three retirements, David and Michael Rattenbury (back from Queensland and still ragging me about last year's grand final) came to the crease together and proceeded to belt the bowling all round.

The last 9 overs took us from 129 to 228. 99 runs off 54 balls. I think we broke them with that.

After tea, Bennie played his usual game. Rats, take us through that first over will you? Was it really 4, 4, 6? Tell us we're dreamin'. But we weren't. They were scoring at 6 an over but we were pretty sure it wouldn't last. It didn't. Bennie went. Caught by one of the Kents. Don't know which one. There are so many I can't remember them all. Elbow came and played beautifully. But not for long enough. Though we put down a couple of catches, we took a few others too. The Eagles had three bats in good form – Tatts got 40 – but were down on their grand final form and team. And they had a few injuries which gave us an edge.

By drinks, and even though they were over the ton, I don't think anyone doubted we had them. Rats, David, Tex and John Kent had bowled very well and we were on top. Roger and Dean took over and both bowled well. We endured the usual farce of a batter with a runner.

Wickets fell at regular intervals, as wickets do. By the 32nd over, I was sharing the bowling around. Craig Kent, Gary Gavin, Michael Kent and Paul Grant all got a go and picked up the remaining wickets between them. Paul got two in the last over, depriving me of a bowl.

Eagles all out for 157. In the end, we probably let them get more runs than they deserved. Still, a win against the team that defeated you comfortably only 4 games ago is pretty satisfying.

Canterbury by 71 runs.

We have now scored 630 runs in three games and have lost, I think, 13 wickets.

We have refreshed the team with three new players (Bob Angley, David Hastings, Michael Kent) and altered the batting order. We can be optimistic about the rest of the season. But, and remember this, there is no room for hubris.

Next match is a fortnight away. At Mont Albert.

A Little Less Comfortable Over 50As, CCC v Mont Albert, Hislop Park, North Balwyn

20 November, 2011

OK, let's get one thing out of the way right from the start. Yes, I was out first ball. No, it wasn't unplayable; I just wasn't up to it. No, I wasn't the only one. The other Golden Duck – Paul Grant – will remain unidentified.

Glad we've put that to one side.

Now. To the business of the day. Yes, we won again. A little less comfortably than we might have thought. But we still won. Them, 9 for 131 (one retiree). Us, 6 for 135 (one retiree) off a bit less than 32 overs. 'Efficient' would be an apt description.

They batted first, after their captain and I had metaphorically tossed over the phone on Friday when he asked if they could bat first as their wicketkeeper was arriving late. True story.

Mike Rattenbury opened for us and had a success in his second over. An LB. Well, yep, it may have been a long way down the strip and could easily have bounced over the stumps; but the opening bat was still out. Along with Brian Clarke, Rats kept a tight rein on the batting and the pressure was on them the whole time.

They only got away from us in one over, a tenner. Otherwise, the Rattenbury/Clarke combination conceded only 28 off 11 of their 12 overs.

The second wicket fell at 51, the third at 89 and the fourth at 115. So, they had a couple of good partnerships and a 40 retired.

Tex was his usual stingy self. 1 for 5 off 6 overs, including 3 maidens. You can't buy that kind of pressure. Well, you can, but we can't afford it.

The medium pacers copped a bit. Kent J and Paul Grant gave up 48 between them off 9 overs. We dispatched them to the naughty corners at fine leg and long off to think about their futures.

After that, we changed the pace a bit. Some speed, with Mark Watkinson (2/17), Roge (slower, above the eyeline, serviceable, unlucky) and the other Kents, who got 4 for 3 between them. In the end, the Mont Albertians lost 5 for 16. All out 131 off marginally fewer than the allotted overs.

What a difference a catch makes. I reckon half a dozen catchables went within a long hand of being picked up. We pick up a couple and I reckon they're out for 100.

As it was, we caught five with Gary G, keeping for the first time in four years, getting three. Tom who? Bob who?

Then we batted. Second over. First ball. Paul was back inside having a cup of tea and mumbling as he went. I should be a bit kinder. Michael 'The Other' Kent was injured (old man's injury, a calf) and I prevailed on Paul at the last minute to open.

Gary G was still in and continuing his great form. Craig 'Yet Another' Kent was helping him out and stayed until the score was a respectable 39. A good 20 from YA, with a truly great shot that was a pull straight down the ground.

With Gary's eventual retirement at 40, we didn't lose another wicket until 116. Kent J got 30 before he was out to a skyed shot that was meant to be a six straight down the ground and Tex got 23 in a very controlled knock.

Did I mention how good the bowling was? Some of those guys could have played in the Mont Albert second XI or at least the Over 40s (if we'd not agreed to shift the match back a week).

Now, I've already talked about the next wicket and it doesn't merit any further elaboration.

We lost one more wicket – Watto for 8 – good effort; before the opening bowlers got us home with a final big hit four from Clarkie.

It was a bit less comfortable than expected but the bowling was good and J Kent and Tex did very well to deal with the brunt of an at times pacy and always tight attack. Very satisfying.

What did we learn? Catches do make a difference. (We knew that.) Watto is recovering his youthful form. (He knows that.) Rats is a very capable bowler. (He told us that. Geez, he fields well off his own bowling.) We can succeed against good bowling. (Good to know that.) A first ball duck sucks. (Just ask Paul and me.)

Wipeout
Over 50As, Eley Park v CCC, Blackburn South

5 February, 2012
Washout, actually.

What can I say? EPCC won the toss and batted, as we would have done. They made 197, as we would have done, at least. We took few wickets and they'd have taken fewer. We made 30-odd without loss before the rains came. They'd have been 4 for 30 in our position.

It always disappointing to be washed out.

All in all, I'd rather have had a chicken sandwich.

Seriously, they had some good batters and I can see why they score heavily.

But the conditions – hot northerly, can't hear yourself think – were totally against the bowlers so little can be gauged from Sunday's game. I actually thought our fielding was reasonably good.

Will be interesting to see how EPCC go against Mitcham. We play Tamil Athletic, at home, on turf. The bowler boys have been itching to play on turf all year. Now they can. Go you bowlers.

Playing Tamil Athletic

February 2012
Another note to my cricketing colleagues.

Well boys, there is a very interesting comparison to be drawn between us and the Tamils.

Us	**Them**
2nd highest scoring team in the competition	Lowest scoring team
2nd highest runs against	Least runs against
Least wickets lost	2nd least wickets lost
Most wickets taken	Least wickets taken

The overall thing this tells us is that we are a very attacking team and they are very defensive.

We have a clear advantage in batting and that will be the biggest thing in our favour: we can outscore them if, collectively, we play to our year's form.

And while they seem unlikely to take too many of our wickets, they look like they will be good at restricting our score. That they haven't taken a lot of wickets suggests their ability to limit scoring means defensive fields and good fielding. We saw evidence of both when we played them early in the year.

It also tells us that we should not give our wickets away easily because that will limit our major batting advantage: we score quickly but losing wickets quickly will make us conservative.

So, steady batting is the order of the day, at least initially. Steady batting will ensure we don't lose wickets rapidly. And steady batting will also mean we take advantage of their weakness: an inability to take wickets. That approach should leave us with plenty in the tank for a late flurry.

So, on the batting side, it looks like **business as usual** will get us enough runs even if their fielding did succeed in limiting us a bit. I reckon we should be aiming for at least 200, even if their fielding is good.

One final batting point: their opening bowlers were very economical in the home and away game: 26 off their 12 overs. We shouldn't worry too much if they repeat that effort; but taking all the singles will be to our advantage. We really shouldn't let them limit us to 26 off the first 12 overs.

On the bowling side, our wickets come at a cost: teams tend to score heavily against us. That should not be a big drawback on Sunday because the Tamils are not a big scoring team and because we take wickets.

But I think we should be aiming for economy on the bowling side and better concentration and effort in the field. We'll take note of where the openers want to hit the ball early and may not keep a slip for very long.

Last time we played, they batted first and got 9 for 151 off 36.

They started brilliantly but lost five quick wickets to be 5 for 59. They did well to get to 151.

We lost some early wickets but good innings from Bob Angley, Kent J and Paul Grant got us home comfortably.

We passed them with 4 wickets down at the end of the 32 over.

So, a comfortable win. 4 overs is a good margin batting second.

Our usual opening bowlers didn't play. They will this week.

This week: we'll bat if we win the toss, take singles to break up the opening bowling attack, but play our usual game, steady at the start with room to move later. Four good innings and we should get to 200.

When bowling, just be a bit tighter, especially early; take all the catches and follow the basics in the field. Same if we bowl first.

Remember (#1), at least some of the Tamils are vegetarian; so please, don't all of you bring ham sandwiches for afternoon tea.

Remember (#2), the Trivia Night is Saturday night. The Legends should be able to put up at least one table. I'll be there in time to put a marker on a table. Let me know if you have forgotten the details.

Remember (#3), all of you – 14 – have qualified and we want you all there.

Lazy Sunday Afternoon Over 50As, CCC v Eley Park, Canterbury Sports Ground

Grand Final, 26 February, 2012
I could feel the nerves building all week. It wasn't just me. Gary Gavin had sent me an email about the batting order. Kent J's injured leg was on everybody's lips. The Mailman wanted a meet and several of us, including David, met and had a beer. Eley Park wanted to talk early starts. We were all following the weather forecasts. It was, as The Phantom says, all happening.

Grand Finals are like that.

Have you seen *Ferris Bueller's Day Off*? And how people kept asking Ferris' sister how he was? My week was like that. People in the streets of Balwyn and Canterbury would stop and ask how we would go and wish me luck. Save Canterbury. True story.

Sunday finally arrived. (What a cliché. Did I write that?). Eventually, the day does arrive and you play.

My prep is to be meticulous about the gear and the meat for the after-match BBQ. I am not so much the captain as the catering manager. Gary Gavin is meticulous too. Did you see him lining up the boundary cones just so? The rest of you seem more relaxed, though I reckon Tex is a seething mass of cricket emotion inside that sceptical exterior; and inside Dean I'm sure there's a really loud high-fiver just waiting to be liberated.

Things seem to just materialise. Francis and Tom come along and things happen. The bar opens, mysteriously. Suddenly, there are more tables in the Jean Green room. A crowd arrives, but it's theirs. A large branch falls from one of the gum trees out the back. I'm trying to interpret that metaphysically. A good omen or bad?

I'm itching to toss because I've come to think the toss is the key to a game between two big hitting sides. And I saw how the Tamils dealt so badly with the pressure that comes from chasing a big score. I desperately want to bat.

John, EPCC's skipper, and I meet. He has been examining the pitch in minute detail. Checking the camber of the grass, the exact angles of the creases, the shine on the bails.

We shake hands. It's grim. The umps wish us well and produce the coin, which I toss and John calls heads. Wrongly. Once again, I win the toss, as I have in the four GFs in which I've captained CCC. Once again, I bat. (Well, actually, I bowled once and we lost).

I'm beside myself. We have a real advantage.

Kent J is playing and we don't need to change the higher order. GG and Mikey K go in. They start confidently but we are startled by Mike's calf injury. I run for him. As it happens, the injury is a blessing. With no other option, Mike goes the tonk with great success. Several fours and a six just gush from his flashing blade (OMG, did I write that!). At the other end, Gary is carrying on from last week. Eventually, Mike gets out but we are sixty-nine and only ten overs have been bowled.

Inevitably, Gary gets another 40. Shots to every part of the ground. If only we had his batting map. What a finals series he has had.

EPCC's bowlers are all over the place. Charlie Green has bowled OK but Crowie and the others bowling into the wind are spraying them everywhere. Lots of wides. The umps are a bit tough, we think, but they seem to know what they're doing.

With Gary retired, the two other Kents are at the crease. The momentum continues. By the time John is out (for 30), we are 142 and thinking 250 might be possible. We are even more confident of that as Craig gets to 41. The first four batters have accumulated 141 between them and that would usually be enough to win any game. But we do not underestimate EPCC.

Off the field, we are now worrying that we might score so fast we will be all out before the 36th over. Not hubris; just more nervous energy.

Rats, promoted in the order, plays over the top of one and is out for 6 with the score at 162. Paul Grant is being cautious as he and Tex (13) take us to 189 for 4 including two retirements.

Enough? Not quite.

Paul and I settle into a partnership with the main topic of inter-over conversation being when he will unleash. But he doesn't need to as their eighth bowler presents enough opportunities for him to score. At the other end, Queeny is on the spot until I surprise everyone – including me – by hitting him for six.

Then, Paul runs me out going for the second run as he reaches 40. A double play. Five for 240. Bob, David and Clarkie take as to 245, the highest score I can recall in my Canterbury Legends career. Enough? We're not home yet.

They have an injured opener but he doesn't suffer long as Rats removes his off bail in the first over with a brilliant piece of craftsmanship.

But they can bat and proceed to do so. Sully and their number three are moving things along quite smartly so I decide to save Rats for the end game. Clarkie is pretty tight on what is a paradise for batters. His six overs for 26 is very good on this pitch. Likewise, Tex, six overs for 29. Paul, taking over from Rats, takes a bit of stick and I change him out. Likewise Gary. Bowling into the wind is a challenge today.

After 15 overs, they were 90, same as us.

Changing the bowling seems to work reasonably well. David comes on and gets a wicket and, as ever, Roger bamboozles them for just long enough to get one too. A great stumping by His Bobness.

Despite a couple of difficult dropped catches, our fielding is very good. We had a few blokes on the boundary, as was merited by the state of the pitch and EPCC's good batting. Just as well the Parkers didn't put their blokes deep early.

Watto is working very hard on the boundary and is causing them a great deal of frustration as he continually cuts off fours. At the end of the day, he looked exhausted but was so effective he even got congrats from the umps. Likewise, Gary and Craig were superb.

The Parkers are slower in the middle order but are still scoring quite freely. Hawko is getting a few but we still have tricks up our sleeve. Another stumping from Bob and a run out by Paul. Paul – promising big things after his pretty ordinary early spell – and John – promising the world, as usual – both live up to their promises and tighten things up bowling their darts. With 4 overs to go, they need 60.

We were been under a little pressure in the middle 12 overs but bounce back during the final 12. Rats and John share the last four overs as we win, with relief, by 36.

We win in the fashion we played throughout the year: fast, high scoring from talent spread throughout the order; tight bowling, especially from our three main bowlers, Rats, Clarkie and Tex; fine back up bowling with enough options to bring both surprise and variety to the game; very good fielding when it counted; and a good team spirit that not even KRudd could dampen. Canterbury, you're great!

Thank you all. Best wishes.

Cricket, It's a Gamble Over 50As, North Balwyn CC v CCC, Macleay Park, North Balwyn

14 October, 2012
Yes, it's a gamble alright.

To gamble is to take risks in the hope of some kind of gain.

The question is: how big a risk do you want to take given the trade-off between risk and reward?

This is a difficult because everybody's perception of risk is different and everybody's assessment of the value of the reward tends to be different too. So, weighing risk and reward and deciding what to do is a complex calculation, especially in cricket when the variables are endless.

The first gamble of the day is the toss of the coin. What a classic case of a gamble. 50/50 chance. Doesn't matter how many times you toss the coin. Doesn't matter how many heads or tails have come up in a row in umpteen previous tosses. The chance of a head or a tail is 50 per cent each and every time. In the jargon, this is because each toss is independent of every other toss.

I called heads. And won the toss again. Is this skill or chance? I usually claim skill at toss-winning; but that's a vast exaggeration.

We bat. Batting first slices the odds, I reckon, in a one-day game. Nothing to do with chance. I believe in scoreboard pressure and the best pressure is when you have 260 runs on the board after 36 overs. Not that I was thinking of that when

I tossed with Chris Hochen, North Balwyn's skipper. I thought 200 would be great.

Anyway, I took no chances and Gary Gavin and Bob Angley opened. Risk-free and high reward. They proceed to hammer the bowling. 14 fours between them in their combined total of 80. Both retire at 40.

Goldy hobbles to the crease, recalling that his knee gave way with a crunch like a sandy gear box two years ago at this ground in this match.

He can't run anymore and that's the risk. But he can still bat. And proceeds to. Eight fours in his 40 retired. A higher risk than the fitter players but what a great reward.

Watching Alan run between wickets with Dean Galvin is like watching time stand still. As a matter of fact, I rather like to watch time stand still. And grass grow. And yacht races. And paint dry. Dean's innings was a powerful counter to the risk appetite of the first three. But needed to be. You cut the batting risk sometimes by pairing a steady hand with risk-taking extroverts. Dean did his job. A nice neat picket fence of 8. Dean's was the first wicket to fall, at 157.

Tex was next. His pairing with Dean did not speed up time or even turn it back. Out for 28 runs of lusty hitting. No risk there. 2 for 168.

I was in by this time but Rats, who joined me had, seemed to have most of the strike. A single off most last balls. Good thinking, Mick. Protecting the strike from the slower bat.

But what a good innings. 43 retired with 30 in boundaries and – wait for it – a two!

Paul Grant, who had claimed soreness from his risk taking in the thirds on Saturday, joined me. Actually, I was expecting John Allen and maybe he was expecting to join me too. But somebody clearly made a risk/reward judgement and sent Paul. He played his usual late-in-the-innings innings, with those lovely, risk-adjusted clips off his toes for four. Not out 16. Not out 23 to me.

So, 36 overs, 2 for 260. Has there been a higher score than that in the Legends? Beats our 6 for 254 in last year's season opener. A great start to the season.

I concluded that the risk calculation had fallen in our favour. Was I right? Could Norths score 261?

No, that much was pretty clear after seven overs when they were 22 compared to our 54 after 7.

Let's sum up this risk-fest quickly now. The rest of the game was a bit lack-lustre. Tex was bored. He has a short attention span.

But there were highlights.

Haggs was persuaded to reward himself with a spot in the 50s and bowled beautifully. Jesse McLaren recently described Haggs as the most under-bowled bowler at CCC. No more. Keep up that form, Pete, and you'll be over-bowled before you know it. His spell left nothing to chance. 2 for 16 off 6.

Speaking of chances, 'Sonny' Bill Hansen nearly took a ripper off his own bowling. A dive to a ball down low, on the follow through. If other Legends had that suppleness, we'd take every catch. Now we know for sure that Bill can bowl. Another good-to-watch action and we can be pretty sure (that's gambling talk when you think about it) that Bill's contribution this season will cut the odds as much in our favour as he cuts and swings the ball.

John Allen still has a beautiful action, as risk averse as it is flowing. On turf, he'd be even more risky for batters.

And, GG, 2 for 9.

But the highlight was Deano. Four overs, 3 for 13. One C&B, two caught behind. Great stuff.

Norths, 8 for 126. We win. No risk.

What, you say, no Kents? Yes, no Kents. First game in the living memory of the universe when at least one Kent was not playing cricket somewhere. The question on everybody's lips is: can they force their way back into the team? Well, for a start, they'd have to pay their registration. And so will anybody else.

Well done, Legends. The old foe next match: Eley Park. The risk profile will be more challenging. If ever a team wants to beat us, the Parkers do. The motto for the next two weeks is: no hubris, less risk. Go Buries.

The Upper Hand
Over 50As, CCC v Eley Park, Hislop Park, North Balwyn

28 October, 2012
Cunningly, I lost the toss. I could see immediately the terror of indecision in the eyes of EP's skipper as he falteringly declared they would bat. Already, we had the psychological upper-hand.

And so it proved.

The highlights will suffice:

1. Bill Hansen: 6 overs, 2 maidens, none for 7. Bill put them under pressure right from the start and they never really recovered, even given the caught behind that went in their favour. Bill proved bowlers win games
2. Tex one for 17 (I think) off six. A wicket before Christmas is a real treat for Pete.
3. Paul Grant. Another abstemious bowling performance including three wickets. EP scored very few from the end from which these three blokes bowled.
4. Goldy. Just three overs (his knee, you know). One run, I think and the best caught and bowled you'll see in a long time.
5. JK. Our most expensive bowler but bowled quite well.

The Cavillator, on debut in the big time. A serviceable performance though his inexperience showed. Worth persevering with.

Them, 133 after their 36.

The openers – His Bobness and Mikey Kent – made a very lively start and it soon became clear that we would be very competitive. Bob was out for 10 but we were on the way. Goldy got a quick 18 before playing right over one. That bought the Brothers Kent together and both John and Mike got 40s. One gigantic six from Big M, straight down the ground. Craig got fewer but, hey, it's early.

Gary Gavin got most of the rest of what we needed. It was over after 21 overs of our innings.

A very good win against a side not quite as strong as in the Grand Final last year. Our bowling was really good, considering that the three first bowlers from the first game didn't play. Man of the Match: Bill Hansen for great bowling.

Congratulations to the Forties for a fantastic win. We could feel the enthusiasm across Hislop. Keep at it, young fellas.

Sisyphus
Over 50As, CCC v Forest Hill CC, Forest Hill Reserve

11 November, 2012

Sisyphus was a king in Greek mythology who was punished by being compelled to roll an immense boulder up a hill, only to watch it roll back down, and to repeat it forever.

Writing match reports is a bit like that.

Especially when you have been doing it for several years.

Every second Monday night, whether you feel like it or not; whether or not the day at work has been good or bad; even if you've run out of ideas; and Sunday's game has been as boring as all get out and there's nothing much to say.

You go to the computer and hope a sudden burst of inspiration will grip your brain and the report will flow like a string of fours off Michael Clarke's bat. Mostly it works. Sometimes, it's Tuesday night and nothing has happened.

But then, you might hear a word like 'Sisyphus' and you know that, at least, there's an introduction to the match report, even if the intro has very little to do with what is about to follow.

As in this case.

So, let me get to the point.

The Legends played Forest Hill on a beautiful Sunday afternoon. All I had to do was win the toss, we'd bat for 36 overs and score 300, with a kind of upside-down batting order in which those used to the lower orders went in first; and then I could implement the bowling plan in which JAK and Tex would barely bowl and Roger would get 6 for 9 off six overs and I'd get a chance to bowl a couple of overs of leg spinners. None of that happened.

I lost the toss and they batted; or something like that.

Forest Hill is new to the competition and so, apparently, are some of their players new to cricket. We welcome them. But it explains a lot.

They made 86 for 6 off their 36 overs. 20 of those came from two overs which included 4 byes and 4 leg byes. So, 34 overs for 66 runs.

Get the bowling picture? Bill Hansen six overs for nine (which gives him 12 overs for 16 in two games). Tex, three for nine off five overs. Johnny Allen, bowling offies, 1 for 1 off three. A run out and I got a wicket but not from bowling leggies. We bowled 12 bowlers which I know (now) is illegal but was worth the risk.

Then we batted. 13 overs later, John Allen and Charlie Hall had both made 40s and we had passed them. We played on for 5 overs while Paul Grant and Brian Clarke had a bit of match practice. And that was it.

So, thanks to Sisyphus, you have a match report. And I guess you'll get another in a fortnight.

That took me 20 minutes.

Best in Show?
Over 50As, CCC v Mont Albert Green, Hislop Park, North Balwyn

25 November, 2012
Canterbury Legends shared the Hislop Park pavilion with the Schnauzer Club of Victoria last Sunday.

Personally, I didn't realise there were that any people who could actually go ga ga over a dog breed which had to be shaped and shaved every couple of days so that it looks like it's supposed to. But there you are. There are actually that many people. Makes ageing cricket tragics look almost normal.

Given the Schnauzers, how could I go past 'Best in Show' for this week's theme. Thanks, Deano.*

Crufts is the pre-eminent dog show in the world, held annually in London.

There are four categories of dog breed, apparently: Terrier and Hound, Toy and Utility, Gundog, Working and Pastoral. You can see where this is heading, can't you?

Canterbury's players last Sunday fell easily into these categories. Oh, and BTW, I won the toss after two lost losses in a row, so we batted.

Batting, the openers – Angley and Gavin – are clearly Terriers. Usually, they go for it right from the start, though they were a little subdued this week, with only 11 after 6 overs. The chased everything until Bob was bowled for 21. Gary stayed for a while until he ran himself out for 24.

The next two in the batting order are Goldstein and Grant, true working dogs, Kelpies or cattle dogs, I reckon. They just get on with it in a professional way. And they did, though Goldy must have smelled some Whiskas somewhere 'cause he gave up a pretty simple caught and bowled. He provided one of the day's highlights, like a working dog crawling through a tunnel to round up 10 sheep: a clip off his toes for six over square. 21.

Paul got the day's first 40, after realising that if he put his glasses on, he could probably see the ball. I was at the other end before he put them on and I know what ordinary batting looks like now. But once the glasses were on, he played as straight as a Pointer's snout.

I was the day's Toy, batting like I was chasing my tail. Kicked the ball on to my stumps following through a missed pull shot. Bowled, 15.

I want to make a Gundog joke later so nobody gets to be that now. Suffice to say, Tex gnawed away like a dog at a bone, getting to 35 with 7 fours.

Bill Hansen continues to surprise us. He's a rare breed. When he turned up for training pre-season, he said he was a number 11 bat. Well, I wish all our blokes batted like him at number 11: 41 retired, six fours and a six to get over the line. He was our Gun. There it is; the Gundog joke.

Finally, the tail wagged (ha ha) with Watto, Dean and Laurie getting a solid 10. We finished at chew chew chew. Now, this is a quite good Richie Benaud/dog combined pun.

Then we bowled and again it was easy to classify the bowlers.

Laurie, what a mongrel! Opened the bowling and was unplayable. Broke a stump. Got 3 for 14. We'll never hear the end of it. Terrific effort, Laurie. Keep it up and we might select you for the finals. They were four for 16 after 9 overs and, to be honest, the winners' ribbons were already awarded.

Most other breeds got a wicket: Bill, Watto, Dean and Tex. In act of wanton selfishness, I bowled one over. (There you go, Laurie, used your line.) Pity they got to 7 for 125 after being 4 for 16.

The test for us is to stay focussed even though the match is over, as it was after Laurie's opening spell. I can only suggest that we were distracted by the prospects of being 'best in show' later in the season. We'll see.

Ruff ruff!

(* 'The best in show idea was me!' Text from Laurie Cavill)

A Chink in Our Game Over 50As, CCC v Victorian Stars, Hislop Park, North Balwyn

13 January, 2013

I admit it. I am sometimes oversensitive. Really? Yes, I am.

So when I read that our narrow loss to East Donny – they passed us with one over to go and one wicket standing – had revealed a 'chink' in our game over which our opponents were 'salivating' – I knew we had to kill off that myth pretty quickly.

The only thing which would satisfy me was a big win over the Vic Stars and our rightful place back on top of the ladder.

Selection turned problematic. From a field of 16, we were reduced to 13 as Tex preferred the bright lights of Sydney to an afternoon on Hislop Park.

Then we lost the toss and found ourselves fielding. There went the chance of a big boost to percentage on the back of a huge run total.

Our opening bowlers were tight from the start and the first three overs were maidens. Then the game began to unfold in much the same way as our last game against the Stars. Their openers are good batters and took the score to 57 with some very accomplished play against good bowling from the Cavillator and Billy Hansen.

Roger bowled the 13th over and things began to happen. 0 for 57, 1 for 57, 2 for 57, 3 for 57, 4 for 60 something.

First, Goldy ran one of the batters out with direct hit. His Bobness stumped another after a well-flighted Bryce delivery.

Paul Grant took a catch on the boundary off another Roger ball. Next over from Watto, Kent J took a catch at forward square. And then Dean took a blinder at short mid-wicket off Roger.

Roger was a complete mystery to the Stars and finished with 3 for 19 off his six overs. Watto also bowled very well for 1 for 22 off six.

But the Stars kept shining (very bad pun) and eventually rang up 167 for 8. Our bowling was not incompetent, quite the opposite. The Stars played well and the ground ran fast. Goldy brought some life to the bowling late in the innings and got a couple.

Laurie Cavill got 6 for 13. (No, he didn't. But I wanted to say that to make up for all the times I forgot to recognise his great efforts. And he did splay the stumps of one unfortunate batter).

The big difference in our grade is the fielding. If players stop every ball that comes directly to them with a standard fielding technique (USE TWO HANDS), then the team saves 20 odd runs in the field. That is more important than taking every catch.

Apparently, at age 50+ this maxim is very difficult to remember. But I am sure that some deep mediation combined with thoughtful sledging will cure the problem.

Gary G and Bob Angley opened the batting in just the fashion I could have hoped for. Bob was hitting everything and was unlucky to get out in the high thirties. Gary got another 40 not and Kent J, back from the charms of Ecuador, also got 40.

At drinks we were 90 odd and looking good. We lost a couple of wickets (Paul G and Charlie Hall for moderate scores) and were 3 for 152 with plenty of overs to go.

At this point, it is necessary to say that 'cricket is a funny game'. Suddenly, we were six wickets down. Kent C was caught at third man. I went second ball and Lawrie went first ball. We were 6 for 166 which was really 8fa after two retirements. Dean had to put his gear back on and pad up to become the last man standing.

Still one behind.

Watto played out a maiden. Goldy scratched around until he hit the four that won the match.

A chink? I don't think so. Nerves? I'll admit to that. Room for improvement? You bet. Need I say it again? Fielding.

Next match away to West Ivanhoe to decide who gets top spot. You know what we have to do.

Legends Ascend Bodily into Heaven
Over 50As, CCC v West Ivanhoe, Hislop Park, North Balwyn

Grand Final, 3 March, 2013
Frankly, I don't know that there are too many Catholics in the Canterbury Legends team. Canterbury sounds just too Protestant, too liberal, too guilt-free to be home to too many left-footers. Just look at Rattenbury, he's as guilt-free as they come. So, few Catholics. Apart from Goldstein. Yes, believe it or not. And me. Lapsed.

But it doesn't matter; because the Legends win in the Grand Final today confirmed that Catholic doctrine is well and truly alive. For the record, the Legends won 169 to 154 against a spirited West Ivanhoe Uniting.

So, what were the three doctrines on display today? And why does the Legends win prove them?

First, Papal infallibility.

Yes, it's true and it always been true that the Canterbury captain – that is, me – is infallible once he and his apostles cross the Jordan and enter the promised land of the Canterbury Oval.

Now, Grand Finals tend to see people cast doubts on the infallibility doctrine but I know I'm right and always have been right. Notwithstanding the schismatic John Kent. But thanks to John and Paul Grant (always trust a man with two first names) and everybody else who just knew that the mid-on was too deep/not deep enough/too fine/too square and didn't flinch to tell me. But the mid-on wasn't too deep/not deep enough/too fine/too square. At all. It was just right. Papal infallibility is proved again. We won, didn't we?

Second, transubstantiation. You all know what that is, right? I don't have to explain, do I?

We saw this occur many times this afternoon, including some real blood. Dean, bowling fearsomely, got one to bounce so monstrously it anointed a batter's nose after the ball got a top edge and the batter had a rush of claret. Truly, wine was turned into blood. But he returned on the third day – a couple of overs later, anyway – but, sadly for WIUCC, there was to be no resurrection, no salvation. But neither were they cast into the seventh circle of Hell for all eternity (with the French). In fact, they played pretty well, not without blemish but with a believer's determination and surety. But we still won.

Third, the difference between venial and mortal sins.

There were some mortal sins today but the less said about those the better. Frankly, if I'd not confessed vicariously (to the Supreme Umpire) and sought forgiveness collectively (from St George of Ivanhoe), we might have joined the French in the seventh circle. A captain's job is never done. Just remember that. You know what I'm talking about.

There were several venial sins committed including a couple of pretty ordinary efforts at catching but nothing that could not be fixed with a not-to-challenging penance and change in the field placing. Really, the fielding effort today deserved some indulgences and 1000 years off purgatory. So, not too many mortal sins, no unforgiveable venial sins.

Catholic doctrine is safe.

And Canterbury won. That made it three from five consecutive Grand Finals. The last two on the trot. Not a bad record.

We won, I think

1. Because Bob Angley batted very well again even though he later confessed he's not really an opener

2. Because John Kent overcame the setback of his truly awful batting and lack of timing to eventually score 40 – a prodigal son returned
3. Because the Middle Order, who are mainly The Other Kents, made fine contributions, like the usually unrecognised sacristans who set the church flowers and sweep up forgotten eucharists
4. Because the bowling was brilliant:
    - Laurie made a great return at the end to pick up a couple of wickets and – yes, I think I can nearly say it – won the match for us; Redemption Unveiled
    - Peter out thought the batting today to pick up a couple; Goodness Rewarded
    - Rats also returned after an indifferent opening spell to help seal the game – A Sinner Forgiven
    - Billy Hansen – how lucky we are to have him – who bowled so well all season and did so again today. Sainthood Beckons
    - Because of all the fielders, good Apostles that they are.

The match seemed like a struggle between good and evil, with the game in the balance for nearly 40 days and 40 nights. Their run rate was slower than ours and several times we looked like we had cracked it. And while we did not suffer the sin of pride when things turned in our favour; we looked heaven-ward a number of times when things were not going our way. But WUICC kept coming until the very end when the sun broke through the clouds and shone brightly on the Legends. We won.

Your captain, not unlike his papal counterpart, has relinquished his seat. Now, there is a *sede vacante.* I remain, I am told by Goldstein, Emeritus; as we search for some new captainal recipient on whom to bestow greatness.

Bless you.

Statistical summary 2012/13

I hate to go on about this; but here were some truly great efforts by the Legends players this year. Here are the highlights:

Batting

1. Bob Angley 200 runs at 33
2. Gary Gavin 164@41
3. John Kent 161@161
4. Michael Kent 151@75
5. Alan Goldstein 139@27
6. Paul Grant 130@43
7. Special mentions: Bill Hansen's only innings for the season, 41 ret; Dean Galvin's fine late innings whirlwind against East Doncaster; Craig Kent's two finals innings of 25 and 26 scored at great pace.

Bowling

	0	M	R	W	Av	ER
Bill Hansen	54	4	162	4	40.5	3
Peter Mirkovic	53	7	135	12	11.25	2.5
Michael Rattenbury	24	0	95	7	13	4
Laurie Cavill	38	5	143	7	20	4.3

Great efforts by Tex and Bill who conceded only 33 runs between them from 12 overs each game. Tex's 12 wickets at

11 shows his great season. Bill should have had more wickets and would have with a little more luck. And Rats and Laurie with 14 wickets between them and real economy. I think the bowlers won us many games that the batters had set up.

Special mentions: Roger's 3 for 19 against Vic Stars who had no idea how to play him and Dean's 3 for 13 in the opening game of the season. Something usually happened when Roger or Dean came on.

Finally, Bob Angley was the champion player of the Legends competition. Apart from his 200 runs, he took 14 wickets behind the stumps, including an outstanding 5 stumpings.

Well done, all. Well done, Bob; and congratulations.

Veterans Ashes Tour, 7 to 24 August, 2013
Opening the Bottle
Wine Trade Sports Club Cricket Club v CCC
Hampton Wick Royal Cricket Club,
Hampton Wick, London, England

9 August, 2013
There is a point in any adventure when the adventure actually starts. When all that has to be done to plan the adventure has been done. When the only thing left is the doing. CCC reached that point on 9 August when we took the coach from London to Bushy Park to play our first game of the 2013 Ashes Tour.

We were all impressed by the ground, the pitch, the weather and especially ourselves as we conducted the mandatory pitch inspection and made erudite commentary ('hmm, yep, that's a pitch'); with a determination to be as congenial as possible to HWRCC, our hosts and to the Wine Society, our opponents. As the captain for this game, I was obliged to wear the 'Hickey'. Our affectionate name for the CCC blazer – the box with buttons – that club president, Tom Hickey, has provided for captains to wear at the toss.

In the Northern Hemisphere, a coin spins in the opposite direction to its spin in the South; just like water down a plug hole. So, I called tails instead of heads and, of course, I won the toss. We batted, on a flat, hard pitch.

Lacking imagination, I put Gavin and Angley in to bat, as I have done for the past two domestic seasons. Lacking imagination themselves, they proceeded to score runs instead of doing something different.

The Wine Society produced a corker of an opening bowler, a left armer with a bit of swing, one piece of which got past His Bobness' bat to his pad and Bob was given out. In an extraordinary act of re-corking, Bob was recalled. It will remain a mystery whether he hit it or not; but he was back and proceeded to reward this act of forgiveness by playing every imaginable shot to get himself out, which he eventually did, for not many.

The brought Greg P to the crease and he proceeded to play beautifully, hitting the ball high and wide and straight and square. Alas, our joy was brought to a premature end with Greg out at 22. He has so many shots he has difficulty deciding which one to play. If I were philosophising, as I sometimes do, I'd recommend Seneca to him: follow the line of least resistance and do the obvious.

Gary Gavin, no longer lacking batting confidence, continued to scamper up and down the pitch. Yes, he's a scamperer, legs like pistons, helmet bobbing as a buoy in a mildly agitated sea. Lots of pulls and cuts and that slightly untidy shot he tries to play behind square to a ball drifting to leg. Gary set the day's standard with a fine 31.

Adam P has no self-doubt. Philosophising again, I think of Nietzsche, all swagger and Ubermensch. On this occasion, swagger and Ubermensch did not translate into that many runs. Nietzsche wouldn't have cared. He'd just shrug his shoulders and swagger anyway. I'm guessing Adam has a few more runs coming soon.

Then we were into the middle order and one can't help being reminded of the Australian XI. Kent M, Kent C and Angwin had all the resilience of Shane Watson, all the confidence of Usman Khawaja and all the promise of Steve Smith. I think we got about 20 between us.

At this point, we were still confident of a reasonable score and John Kent, as ever, promised to get us one. I can't remember how many he scored and at 530am, as I am writing this, I'm not knocking on any doors asking for the scorebook. It was more than 20 but less than 30.

Charlie Hall, in a valuable late innings got a few with J. Allen contributing a final flourish from a single ball.

157 was a respectable score though I think our commonly-expressed view that it was 'competitive' was commonly-expressed more in hope than anticipation.

Yet, after 20 overs, they were behind the pace at 2 for 68 and I think we thought we had a chance. And we had tickets on ourselves when they were 3 for 85 after 26.

Their captain was batting well but we had taken a few wickets and with the sun shining and a gentle breeze blowing we might actually have believed that we were heading to our rightful place in cricket history: the first win of a nine-match whitewash.

Hubris. I've spoken of this before. It goeth before a fall and it didth again.

One should never assume anything about anything. Beware that tall, awkward fellow who plays cross bat shots. Robin Florent-Flockhart. Remember that name.

TWS – you can work that out – had upped the pace a bit by hammering some of our pace bowlers ('pace' may be an overstatement) so we decided to take a bit of pace off the ball and brought Mikey Kent on. Mistake. Not Mikey's. Mine. Three big sixers in an over from that tall awkward fellow who plays cross bat shots and the game was now in the balance.

We were told HWRCC had to get tilers in from time to time to replace tiles broken by tall awkward fellows playing cross bat shots that crack the ancient tiles on the clubrooms. They had to do that again after our visit.

In the end, they got the necessary 158 with plenty to spare. Did I mention that I dropped a dolly of a catch off Gary Gavin?

Clarkey was the pick of our bowlers. His 8 overs for 20 with a wicket repaid all the hard work he did pre-season. He was superb. Johnny Allen bowled well and it's great to have a tall quick bothering the openers. JAK and Rats got a wicket each.

Adam P was our little bowling surprise to ourselves. An Ubermensch is never beaten.

The after match was pretty impressive and our hosts provided some exotic and excellent wines to celebrate the game. We were made very welcome.

Now stories like this often end with something like 'so, tired and sunburned, the boys headed for home, satisfied they had done their best'. Well, something like that. Except, that back at our hotel the party raged and the martinis became the drink of the Tour.

I can't end this report without comment on the enthusiasm and support of the non-playing Tourists, the WAGS, and their photographic endeavour to provide the Tour's visual record and the levity that busted our hubris. The role of partners is sometimes to bring reality to the exaggerated view we have of ourselves. And believe me, the view we have of ourselves is exaggerated.

The Captain's Burden Oxford Downs Cricket Club v CCC Standlake, Oxfordshire, England

12 August 2013

By Greg Powick (with a little help from Michael Angwin)

Bruce Anderson. Now, there's a bloke who doesn't know when to shut up.

I love him but, geez, can't he let it rest a bit. He goes on and on about my intensity. He goes on and on with allegations that I 'overthink' the game. Doesn't he know that cricket, especially batting, is not just a game but a lifestyle.

Glad I got that off my chest.

Let me tell you a bit about my approach.

Captaincy. You don't know what a burden it is. You have to make speeches. You have to soothe egos. You have to pick the batting order. And when bowlers bowl. You have to decide when your brother bats. And when you bat yourself.

And this is a declaration game.

How am I supposed to remember all these things? 'Declaration' game means you have to decide when to declare with just enough to give the other lot the thought they can get them in the time remaining.

In the end, you have to take a deep breath and just get on with it. Well, I'll do the captaincy once, give Bruce a few platforms for his inexhaustible undergraduate good humour and then just get on with playing. It'll all be over soon.

Batting order. Well, Adam and I better open. Or should I bat first drop? Stocky #3? Or maybe Charlie? I s'pose Bruce will have to bat somewhere but not with me, I hope. What am I going to do?

I guess I'll have to bite the bullet.

I won the toss and had to wear that damn blazer. It's so embarrassing. Another of a captain's burdens. Yes, Adam and I will open. But he can face, I think.

He gets a leg bye and I'm facing. The ball hits me on the pad. I'm out. Oh, the horror! I told you the captaincy was a burden but at least the team's expectations won't be so high. What a relief.

Stocky looks good at the crease but is also out LB. 2 for 25. Francis gets a duck to a ball from a left-handed young fella that he leaves and watches take his off stump. I'm not kidding: Francis is at least 50 years older than this kid who is about three foot tall. 3 for 25.

How embarrassing can this be.

This brings Dalts to the crease and he and Adam proceed to build a great partnership. Both are batting beautifully. Forget the details just focus on the big picture. They take us to 4 for 150 in 21 overs. Adam gets 81 and Dalts 59. I love cricket like this even when I'm not making the runs.

When Dalts gets out Bruce gets in. Another relief. He's been in my ear for an hour. I hope he has a long innings so I can get some peace and quiet.

Luckily for me and the team he does. I guess all the energy will have to burn off somehow. Better that it is via his batting rather than all the time he has on his hands to do nothing but Tweet, whatever that is. Wish he'd never heard of it.

Charlie Hall bats elegantly for 23 not out and Lindsay Gates get 11 not out at the other end. We get to 258 off 40 overs with seven wickets down.

Their quick has taken 3 for 21 off six in a very good performance.

Well, we are now about to learn a bit about cricket. These blokes are very good.

Oxford Downs' opening bats take just 17 overs to peel a ton off our bowlers, most of it in boundaries. All our bowlers are dealt with severely. Johnny Allen gives up 48 from 8, Billy Hansen 72 from 11 and Bruce 23 from 3. I hope that shuts him up. Fond hope. Johnny and Bill, at least, get a wicket.

But Dalton is our best bowler today with 3 for 45 from 10 on the trot.

While we get their number 3 for a duck, numbers 4, 5 and 6 get 43, 36 and 31.

With six overs to go, they need 51 to win. They go about getting them with ease and confidence. They need 2 off the last ball but they get only 1.

It's a draw but good enough to be a tie. How impressive were the OD batters as they went about the task of getting the runs. No panic. No rash shots. Lots of experience and talent here. We learn a bit about declaration games but still have a lot to learn.

Once again, lovely ground and warm hospitality. I made a speech – thank God that's over – and it wasn't as cringe-able as I thought it might be. But Bruce still kept talking. Another two weeks of this. Can I cope?

Landscape and memory

I've been reading Ricky Ponting's autobiography. He writes: 'There is something very special about an Ashes tour...It builds a special camaraderie.' That's what the CCC Legends Tour of 2013 did for me; and I reckon it did for the rest of the Tourists too.

The Tour was a long time in the making, getting its initial push just after the 2011/12 season and then getting serious prior to the 2012/13 season. The idea for the Tour came from many sources – apparently – but I think we can settle on Brian Clarke as the *capo di tutti capi* of the Tour idea.

The organisers were initially worried that we might get only 15 takers but, eventually, there were 30 Tourists.

Can I say that having the WAGS along – I hope they don't mind that expression too much – was a fantastic inclusion.

Three weeks of complete cricket blokeyness might have been a Touring nightmare; and the WAGS helped us avoid the Australian Test team's touring normality, which has employed facial hair growth and dress-ups, not to mention homework. As it was, the WAGS were a source of good humour in the face of too much cricket conversation and were a great support – they know how to clap politely, regardless of the circumstances; and they brought a tremendous sense of fun and mickey-taking to cricket tragics who sometimes took themselves oh-so-seriously.

The organisation involved multiple meetings over many months. You'd be surprised at the subject matter and the range of things that need to be considered in planning a Tour; and at the struggle between the 'hands off crew' and the 'planning pedants'.

Fortunately, we had Stuart Stockdale to guide us, though we told him constantly how to organise the Tour. He had, of course, only organised 25 tours before he got to us. We thank him for his patience and his outstanding ability to under-promise and over-deliver. I recall his serious attempt to dampen our enthusiasm for the Royal Hotel at Winchester; then delivered a rip-snorter of an experience there.

The main planning rule – stay as long as you can in one place – worked brilliantly. As Ricky Ponting says, '...you can unpack your suitcase and make yourself more comfortable...'

The other Touring feature that worked brilliantly was the coach. Apart from being a great form of travel for a group like ours, the coach was the scene of pre-match strategy, post-match analysis, carousing and great mirth; and occasionally, competitions (name the Australian Test cricketer whose name begins with Q). The coach was a source of the camaraderie that we built up. So were the multiple meals we ate together, in larger or smaller groups. And the touristing. So was the drinking we shared; responsibly, of course.

But most of all it was about the cricket. We loved it and all of us proved extremely good at it, didn't we?

What can I say about the grounds? That image of the Cowdray Ruins, perfect cricket field with a 17th century castle ruin in the background, lingers warmly in our consciousness. We didn't care too much that we were beaten on grounds like this.

Our record was average: two wins, one tie, one draw and five losses. We met serious resistance from some teams and were genuinely beaten on their terms. The different forms of cricket we played – especially the declaration game – were a revelation and showed how exciting a draw can be, as our game against Warborough showed. I reckon we might have won another couple of games with small adjustments in our play. Competitive fellows that we are, we'd have appreciated that; but we appreciated more the fact we played in such great company, both our team mates and our opposition.

We played to the best of our ability, albeit making sure everyone got a go, just like we do in our domestic competition. There's always a tension between trying your best to win and managing the expectations of all players. The captains did a pretty good job of that.

We encountered some very interesting opponents. The youngest, a 13 year-old, whose mother drove him to a cricket match every day of the summer and who belted us around at Queen's College in Oxford; the 55 year-old coming up for his 1000 runs for the season; the former Australian under 19 captain; the 84 year-old playing his second game in two days; the 17 year-old girl, a likely first class cricketer in the future; the Aussie professional polo player who took 94 off us at the Cowdray Ruins.

But these are only the stand outs. We played against blokes like us, who made us feel truly welcome and played in great spirit, hard and competitive, but friendly.

Our highlights included Adan Powick's high score for the Tour, 81; Greg Powick's and Bruce Anderson's two fifties; John Allen's 5 for 24 as he tried to win us the game at Cowdray; Brian Clarke's 6 for 82 from 25 overs on the trot; Francis Bourke's catch a Middleton Stoney; LG's' sparkling innings at Queen's College. Can I modestly add my own 50 at Warborough?

And who would have missed the opportunity to sledge KP at The Oval?

We discovered a few things: like the fact that Dalton Wegener is a very good captain and Gerg Powick a very anxious one; that The Other Powick has a Big Personality; that Bob Angley's fashion sense stands up to scrutiny; that Kurt Hansen can bowl leggies and keep to a timetable; that Shuggy still has it; that Billy Hansen really can bowl all day; that Mikey Kent's bowling can be hit out of the park; that Charlie Hall must have been a really good cricketer in his youth; that English beer is pretty good at the close of play; and that there is an inexhaustible supply of Kents to call on for any role though it can sometimes be a challenge to keep Craig awake.

Already, there's talk of a 'next' tour. Let's hope we can do that before we get old.*

*In fact, CCC Veterans toured England again in 2015 and 2018.

CCC Legends in Shock Loss Over 50As, West Ivanhoe v CCC, Seddon Reserve, West Ivanhoe

27 October, 2013
Usually, when I write about the first match of the season, I do so in a slightly-less-than-humble fashion, saying how I won the toss, how we scored 160 plus (only a competitive total, I'd say – my lip service to humility) and then about how we proceeded to get a gallant opponent out for 110 with 10 overs to spare. I'd end with an analysis of our prospects for the season which, for the last five seasons, has been a uniformly optimistic and, I might say, accurate one.

So, why am I not writing this tonight? Because I lost the toss, West Ivanhoe made 5 for 154 and we, the gallant opponent, could only get 133 with 9 wickets down. My faux humility is now real humility.

Johnny Allen and Laurie Cavill opened the bowling and bowled very well. Not many wickets but very tight. Johnny got a fantastic 1 for 9 off six.

After 18 overs, West Eye was 1 for 64 and I was forecasting 150 in my head. And that was about what they got. Two of their bats got 40s and a couple of others got high teens. The bowling was reasonably tight though the batters did take to Roger and Paul O'Grady a bit.

Billy Hansen bowled at the end of the innings and got the day's best figures of 3 for 23, thanks to some really good catching. Paul O introduced himself with a very good catch and distinguished himself with a great run out (via His

Bobness). Roger stunned us all with great fielding…he fielded more balls at forward square on Sunday than in his previous five years of cricket.

Bob, Bob, Bob. You went in saying you'd overcome your compulsive hooking. We all made you think of England. Susan cautioned you. You tried one and got dropped. And then you did it again and got caught. Is there a cricketing gulag somewhere we can send you? For some re-education? How about a small electrode inserted into one of your body parts? We look forward to your contrition.

Just as well Mikey Kent doesn't pull compulsively. He got 30 including a giant six which he hit so sweetly we could smell it. And his calves were still intact at the end of the innings. Paul O was welcomed to the Legends at #3, where he batted well for a respectable 11. By this time, I had joined another newbie, Stu Pearce whom, of course, I then ran out in welcome, forgetting that in the over 50s some blokes have cause to worry about their hammies. Sorry Stu.

Johnny Allen came in and went for fewer than one in a dismissal that I think may have gone directly to ground before going straight to slip. Billy, umpiring, couldn't see this; and West Eye genuinely thought it was out. Just one of those things JA. Good sportsmanship to leave without complaint.

But this left us 5 for 70 just after drinks and things looked a little more challenging for the faux humble.

Goldy, minus knee and hip, partnered up with me and we played dourly against good bowling. At 102 with 10 overs to go, we thought we might get there. Unfortunately, with the score at 116, Al got a goody that bowled him. We were still in it at this stage but their bowling was now more challenging with the wicketkeeper having swapped his gloves for leg spin. We will have to learn to play this bloke who bowls slow, has a good wrong 'un and gets bounce. He got 2 for 16 off 5.

Deano left us at 127 and I followed at 129 and, officially, the match was over. As gallant as they are, Bill and Laurie couldn't get the last 20 of the last two overs.

Why did we lose? The bowling was a little loose in the middle (not unexpected early in the season) and we were probably a Kent short in the batting. Interestingly, West Eye have scored 152, 154 and 158 against us in the last three matches. So, we know their capability (and their limits). We scored over 160 in two of those matches and only 133 on Sunday. With a little improvement in the batting, I think we'll be OK. The fielding was exceptional, always a good sign.

Those who couldn't play on Sunday will be first in line next time. BTW, please pay your registration fees.

You Couldn't Invent This Over 50As, CCC v Eley Park, Hislop Park, North Balwyn

24 November, 2013
Roger Bryce, the Legends newest batting superstar, guided the over 50s to its first win of the season against Eley Park yesterday. Yes, Roger Bryce. More on that in a moment.

You have to feel for the Parkers, don't you. They haven't beaten us since Tex was a fast bowler; they won their first two games; we lost our first two games. They probably had high expectations. But we won again.

Reverting to form, I lost the toss and we found ourselves bowling on a grey, rainy day. Did that stop us? No.

On a new pitch, dropped in by Boroondara's cricket helicopter, Johnny Allen and Bill Hansen opened up the bowling. What a performance by these two. JA, six overs, 1/12. Billy, six overs, 1/7. John's removal of their star bat in his second over was a treat. Vicious in-swinger to the left hander, knocking his leg stump out of the ground. What a beauty, on a pitch that has a little more bounce and a lot more latent speed. Billy was nearly unplayable. How many times did they play and miss. One was heard to say that he'd have to be a great player to have edged the one that beat him. Bill was helped out by the senior Kent, who took a blinder in the slips, head high.

There was no relief when Rats and Tex took over. At drinks, they were about 40 and just unable to get the bowlers away. Rats had got their skipper who skied one to His Bobness. To give you some idea of the quality of the bowling, the previous match EP had been one for more than 100 at drinks.

We knew they'd go after us following drinks and they did pick up the pace; but the bowling remained tight. For the last 12 overs, Laurie tied up one end while Deano, Kurt and JAK each bowled two overs from the other. At the end, they were 107, just 60-odd off the last 18 overs. All the bowlers were very good.

Bowling's an unpredictable occupation. Deano couldn't take a trick last match but was well on line and length this time. Good come back, mate.

Bob and Stu Pearce opened the batting and Bob proceeded to play with great confidence, backed up by Stu with great technique. The score raced along under Bob's tutelage, with pull shots to all parts of the mid-wicket V. Then, of course, Bob missed a pull shot and was bowled. We weren't entirely surprised but we did enjoy the innings, Bob.

Craig Kent joined Stu and proceeded to play in that delightfully unorthodox fashion that we all love. He has a great eye and swats bowlers from any length. A quick 20 had us well positioned at 2 for about 50. JAK selflessly gave up his batting spot for Roger who played the innings of his life. It may be unfair of me to say that; but, frankly, I've always thought of Roge as a quirky bowler and only an aspiring batter. Wrong again. What an innings. Fours and sixes to all parts of the ground. And, in an astounding achievement, Roge ran a two. No, I'm not mistaken. When Roger departed for 28, we were three for 80-odd after 20 something overs. While they picked up some wickets (Stu, stumped, after an innings of exquisite patience; me, caught behind trying to hit the winning runs), the honour of winning the match went to Laurie, with a final four.

Not our most scintillating victory but a victory marked by exceptional bowling and some fine batting.

If we can keep up that bowling and get a settled batting order, I think we will be a good chance for finals. Fielding? Was pretty good; but we have to keep at that part of our game.

Well done, boys.

That's the Way I Like It
Over 50As, East Doncaster v CCC, Zerbes Reserve, East Doncaster

2 February, 2014

What makes a good day's cricket for you? Is it a Michael Clarke double century against the South Africans? Nathan Lyon bowling 24 overs and getting 3fa not many? Chin music from Mitch? A KP duck?

I like all of those. But I especially like it when the CCC Legends win the final game of the season in great style and set themselves up for another finals campaign. That's what happened at East Doncaster yesterday.

Yesterday, on cue, at a quarter to one, the wind changed direction and a 40-degree northerly turned into a 27-degree mild southerly. A much better day for cricket. Then I won the toss for only the second time this year and we were able to bat first for only the second time this year. We like to have the runs on the board because our bowlers are just great at putting pressure on a chasing side.

As usual, His Bobness and Gary G opened the batting against tight bowling on a pitch showing a good deal of variability. Bob went early; but I wasn't too bothered as he is playing with great confidence and going for his shots. Anyway, Bob's departure paved the way (what a cliché!) for three entirely enjoyable innings from Gary and the two younger Kents.

Don't get me wrong, Gary. I'm not saying you struggled against good bowling. I am saying that the bowling was good and tight and hard to score from. What I liked about your innings is that you refused to be tied down and took the necessary risks to keep the score ticking over. Sometimes it wasn't pretty and I know you weren't satisfied with all your shots. But it was terrific innings in challenging circumstances. Retired at 40.

Mikey Kent has really taken command this season and his innings yesterday demonstrated that. Good defence, good running between wickets (he and Gary ran a four), great footwork and exciting attacking play that took advantage of the fast running outfield. The bowlers had no answer to Mikey's batting authority. Retired at 40.

Then came Craig. What can I say? Quirky. Innovative. Unorthodox. As someone said yesterday, bowl the same ball to Craig three times and he'll play it in three different ways. I don't think he knows this. Retired at 40.

I enjoyed the batting so much, I didn't take a lot of notice of the state of the game. But this is what it was. 74 at drinks. Then the run rate ramped up. One for 120. A couple of cheap outs (me and the oldest Kent). 3 for 155. Charlie Hall (18 no) and Tex (11no) got 30 off the last 4 overs to take us to 183 for three after 36. A good score given the early tightness of the bowling and the variability of the pitch.

We were confident going into the field.

Johnny Allen bowled as well as ever. He bowled the best ball of the season, I think: one that rose off a length at great pace and ripped through to the keeper, leaving the batter puzzled about why he was still in. He smiled in acknowledgement. The smile lasted a ball 'cause John had him caught in covers next ball.

The other opener took advantage of the pace of JA's bowling, the wind and the fast outfield to get some quick runs. We agreed that we needed to take some pace off the ball and Rats replaced John after four overs.

At the other end, Billy Hansen bowled three miserly overs before they scored from him.

Bill, Rats and Tex slowed the batting right down.

Rats had 8 taken from his first over but then proceeded to bowl 5 overs for 12 runs. Pete got a wicket first ball and conceded only 7 runs from his six overs. Should have been two wickets. One of those LBs was plumb.

East Doncaster was 64 after 18 overs and under pressure with the run rate having started to stop. They were under even more pressure when the opener retired at 40.

Peter McKee came on and took a couple of wickets (he was on a hat trick) with some lively bowling. John Kent and Charlie Hall (one wicket) bowled very economically to keep the pressure up. Laurie Cavill, whose role is to bowl at off stump for six of the last 12 overs, did just that, finishing with one for 20 that should have been two for about 10. Well bowled, Laurie. We all enjoyed your performance. We also enjoyed Bob's athletic keeping.

That's the way I like it.

Not all the results from yesterday are posted yet but I know the Park sides' result: Ainslie beat Eley. So, we probably finish third and will play Ainslie next Sunday.

As I have been saying for weeks, I think we can win the premiership. We've completed the first task – we made the finals. Our second task is to replicate our winning form: the bowlers will create the pressure that will make our batting hard to beat, whether we bat first or second. As ever, the difference in a tight game is fielding, fielding, fielding. We dropped a couple of catches yesterday but our field placement was good and so was our out fielding. We can still tighten up a bit.

There is an opportunity for practice at Canterbury Oval at 11am next Saturday morning. See you there.

I know a couple of players aren't available next week but please let me know if you are available. I think we will have 14 or 15 players. I would like to give everybody who's available an opportunity to take part.

Asymmetry Over 50As, CCC v Ainslie Park CC, Griff Hunt Reserve, Croydon North

16 February, 2014

Sunday's semi-final between Canterbury and Ainslie Park had an asymmetrical outcome. Canterbury was on the thin side of the asymmetry.

We did just about everything right on Sunday. We won the toss and batted. We made 191 losing only 4 wickets. We fielded very well and took some great catches. The bowlers were again exceptional and took six wickets against very aggressive batting. Yet we remained on the thin side. There is probably only one conclusion we can draw from this. A painful conclusion.

The countervailing argument I am searching for is that we lost one of our best bowlers, effectively from his first ball when a high hamstring took him out for the day. Is that enough to avoid the compelling conclusion for our asymmetry? Probably not. A couple of our bowlers will argue – did argue – that they had bad days, hoping to explain our thinness. But I can point to the 93 runs that came from 14 overs from APCC's finest. Every bowler has his bad day.

No, I can't explain the asymmetry except for a conclusion which has the clarity of canine manhood. In a way, it is comforting to know that perhaps we could not have done any better than we did.

How did all this pan out?

Well, as I said, I won the toss. I had toyed with the idea of bowling but couldn't think of a sufficiently good argument to put to the team. So we batted.

His Bobness and Gary G started at a furious pace, 12 coming from the first over. But the wheel was still in spin. 19 runs came from the next 11 overs as we found ourselves in the unusual position of being 2 for 30 after 12 overs. By then, both openers were out for not many. Strangely, I wasn't too worried by this. Don't ask me why. Subdued, yes; but not worried.

The next 12 overs yielded 87 runs. Mikey Kent played another superb innings of seven fours and a six, retiring at 42. Charlie Hall, promoted in the order and perhaps, I detected, feeling a little nervous, also played very well for 29, including five fours. Charlie went with the score at 83 in the 19th over. But his departure didn't slow the pace.

What a pleasure it is to bat with Mikey, as I was lucky enough to do. Inspired by him, I was able to score a few as well, also 42 retired. Johnnnnny Kent played a measured innings (32 not out), keeping the runs ticking over with his good eye for a single. Tex chipped in with six – his only scoring shot – and Johnny Allen got seven at the death. There were 20 extras, mainly leg byes, the result of good leg work when a bat wouldn't do.

We had scored 108 since Charlie departed in the 19th over. Four for 191. A competitive score and one I think would have beaten every other side in the competition on any day. But no one wanted to be complacent against APCC.

JA started in his usual fashion, with a maiden. First ball of the second over, Billy did a hammy, giving up 12 for the over and then leaving. I felt for Bill. We all did.

One of their openers hit some of the best sixers you will ever see, including two off Rats' first two balls, one of which landed on the grandstand roof. Fortunately for us, Dean and Bob combined to catch him behind the wicket off JA, Bob climbing all over Dean to catch one that Dean had knocked up. They were one for 31, early in the fifth over.

John Allen continued with his great spell, finishing with 2 for 9 off his six overs as APCC's run rate slowed significantly. Rats also came back well after his first two balls. Between them, they slowed the run rate and put us back in the game.

Bill's hammy forced us to change our bowling strategy and Peter McKee and John Kent needed to bowl more overs than we planned. They bowled respectably though against good batting; but, all in all, it was a tough day for bowlers.

After 18 overs, APCC were 2 for 88, five in advance of us at our drinks, thanks to their flying start. I thought, however, that we had done very well to hold them to that total at drinks, considering how they pummelled us early.

Another injury, one of our best fielders, Stu Pearce, copped a middle age calf and limped off. This just doesn't happen to us.

The next six overs were good for APCC. They took their score to the mid-130s and with 12 overs to go – 84 balls – they needed 56. Very gettable, even though they had lost a couple more wickets.

By this stage, Charlie Hall and Laurie Cavill were bowling. They were bowlers seven and eight and they were going to bowl out. The next seven overs saw us get back on top and with five overs to go, APCC needed to score at a run a ball to win. They had not done that for some overs and we looked a bit better. More so, when Mikey Kent took a catch which, if taken in a test match, would have been called 'one of the best catches you will ever see'. The catch mattered because it saw the end of a big hitter.

Again, APCC came back, scoring at nearly a run a ball but still bleeding the occasional wicket.

Come over number 35. Laurie, dispensing with the captain's instruction to bowl at top of off, bowled at the stumps and splayed them everywhere to leave APCC 8 for 190 at the end of another terrific spell. Laurie really found his niche bowling six of the last 12 overs in every match since Christmas.

That brought us to Charlie and the last over. Second ball, caught behind! Could it get any closer.

It came down to this: four balls, one run or one wicket. We all came in to save the single.

Then it was over. Their number 11 clipped Charlie off his hip for a single and as APCC needed only a draw to go forward. That was it. We bowled out the over.

Well, boys, we didn't quite make the grand final but we gave it a shake. We'll no doubt talk about this a bit more over drinks and dinner in a couple of weeks; but I think we can reflect on a good season where the teams that beat us have emerged as very good teams.

Congratulations to the Over 40s for making the grand final. The young fellas have learned a thing or two, I think. We'll be there to cheer you on.

I think I can see the twilight.

The Dismissal
Over 50As, CCC v Ainslie Park CC, Griff Hunt Reserve, Croydon North

27 October, 2014
I'm back.

Not so much by popular demand but – and I'm sure he'll acknowledge this – Laurie has far too much on his plate to write match reports as well as practically run the Canterbury Cricket Club.

I am figuring on a few Gough references this week; and I'll start by calling this report The Dismissal, in due deference to those events of nearly 40 years ago, events that only a few of us can recall at first hand. The Dismissal has a kind of politico-cricket resonance, don't you think?

Our new skipper won the toss and, for the third time in three matches against APCC, we batted first. The duumvirate (another Gough reference for the well-informed) of Gary G and His Bobness opened in fine style and took the score to 32 before Gary was out caught (unlike Jim Cairns who was caught out; but let's not go there). Bob followed ten runs later, bringing the two younger Kents to the crease. Sometimes, a younger age is no barrier to success. Alas, on this occasion, that aphorism proved incorrect as both the Kent boys, though starting well, did not fulfil the early promise of success. A bit like Gough's government.

Then, the current and former skippers came together at the crease and there were several – not many but several – sighs of relief as the team felt this maturity and talent would see us recover from a 5 for 65. But leadership skills were, as in Gough's cabinet, no counter to lack of concentration as both men got out to somewhat careless shots. This carelessness is not reminiscent of Gough; but more like his Liberal opposition of the time, who carelessly lost several elections. We also carelessly lost Roger for not many.

Gough's government was nearly saved by some solid, conventional, conservative ministers, Diamond Jim McClelland and Uncle Bill Hayden. So was Canterbury; nearly saved, that is, by its own solid, conventional and conservative elder statesmen, Diamond Charlie Hall and Uncle John Kent. They took the score from 7 for 72 to 127 before Charlie was dismissed for 25. Uncle went on to get 40 not out and, with a last-minute push from Tex, we got to 8 for 155. Competitive? Maybe. We'd find our soon enough.

APCC opened with the guy who belted us in the semi last year and he proceeded to do so again. 16 off Bill's first five balls. But Bill, like Malcolm Fraser, had the last laugh, bowling him with a beauty from the final ball of the first over. Tex popped a second wicket when APCC was 55. But, really, the election was over. Two of their batters got 40s. They played very well and you get the sense APCC knows how to chase. Laurie got another wicket in the 34th over; but APCC won in a landslide, a bit like the '75 election.

We were probably 30 runs short of a competitive total; and I guess we all hope that the top seven bats can get more than 70 between them next match. The bowling was pretty good. Bill conceded only 19 runs over his 6 overs after losing 16 off his first five balls. Tex, 1 for 18 off 6 and Uncle John only gave away 13 runs off his six. The fielding was good.

Disappointing but not without merit. Hmm, definitely like Gough.

Over 60s National Club Championships, Melbourne, November 2014

The Golden Rules of Cricket...And the Role of Exceptionalism

CCC v UNEX

10 November, 2014

There is a golden rule of seniors' cricket.

Read carefully, here it is: when three of your batsmen score 40 or more you win the game.

Why is this true? Because if three batsmen make 40 or more, your team will make about 200, sometimes more; it is rare indeed for two teams to make 200 on the same day. Ergo, you win.

Simple, huh? Well, no.

As Billy Hansen reminded me today, there is a corollary to the golden rule, which I have – in recognition of Bill's blinding insight – named Hansen's Exception.

Hansen's Exception states that when three of your batsmen score 40 or more you win the game, except when four of the opposing team's batsmen score 40 or more. Today, Canterbury Over 60s were the beneficiary of senior cricket's golden rule and the victim of Hansen's Exception.

I should hasten to add that Bill, who scored a splendid 29, incurring a black eye in the process, and took 1 for 26 off his

8 overs, bears no responsibility for the triumph of the Exception named in his honour.

Today was one of those rare occasions when I was to lose the toss and one of those even rarer occasions when the opposition on winning the toss, does exactly what you want them to do. Accordingly, they put us in. Thanks Unex, a team composed mostly of alumni of the University of New England at Armidale, NSW. Please don't ask me to explain this.

Two players played their first games for Canterbury today, Jim Welsh and Rob Redmond. We had a cap presentation ceremony before the game, with the semi-retired Brian Clarke speaking eloquently in presenting the caps. Actually, that didn't happen. I just wanted to work Clarkie into the story line.

Jim and Michael Loy opened the batting and they took the score to a respectable 31 before Michael was caught. I know he was dissatisfied with his score but, really, he has given us great starts in both games so far. The next wicket fell at 62 when Stockers was given out LBW for 9 EVEN THOUGH HE HAD HIT THE BALL. Did I say HE HIT THE BALL? Is that loud enough, Stu?

I joined Jim who promptly got his 40 and retired when we were 74. 40 number one.

Rob Redmond and I proceeded to work the ball around on a fast outfield before I retired at 40 with the score on 120. Forty number two.

Rob and Francis did the same when, with the score at 175, Francis was bowled for 23. Rob then got his 40 which included a mighty 6. 40 number three.

At this point, I mentioned the golden rule to Bill, who outlined for me Hansen's Exception. We both laughed. It could never happen!

Bill went to the crease and belted a quick 29, with two sixes while Shuggy got a rapid 20.

We had added 51 off the last 4 overs and 96 off the last 10. We were pretty pleased with ourselves, I can tell you. Hubris? Maybe. We have talked of this before, usually after a loss. Hmm.

Let me now cut a long story short. Here are the highlights: Unex lost its first wicket at 51, courtesy of Jim, who bowled an opener. Their next wicket fell at 203, interspersed with four retirements at 40. This was Hansen's Exception in flashing neon lights, accompanied by a very realistic rendition of Tchaikovsky's 1812 Overture, complete with real cannon and notably equine-like cavalry.

We got another wicket but the game was probably lost by then, even though we wouldn't have said so.

Our in-the-field highlights were: Bill's 1 for 26 off 8 and Francis' 1 for 36 off 8 together with Michael Loy's brilliant one-handed catch and Charlie Morris' and Stuart's fielding on the boundary. Really, the bowlers did quite well. We just didn't have enough of them.

Tomorrow's a rest day. Can I hear cheering in the background?

We resume hostilities on Wednesday. I'll just ask as many players as possible to come. I've been chastened by too much planning. From now on, I just intend to let the world unfold, as it did today and enabled us to field a team of nine which nearly won a remarkable game.

See you Wednesday.

No Country for Old Men CCC v Victorian Over 60s Cricket Association

11 November, 2014
Something very interesting has revealed itself over the course of three days of Over 60s cricket.

At that level of cricket, the bat rules the ball.

Batsmen can still play straight. They can still play with a semblance of timing. They are assisted by short boundaries and fast outfields. They can take their time. They can even play with moderate injuries. All they need to worry about are singles and the occasional four.

They have all the advantages over the poor, old bowlers.

Bowlers suffer from physical deterioration is a way that batsmen don't. I'm not saying batsmen don't suffer physical decline; but I am saying that it matters more for bowlers. The bowler has to run in and extend his body in an unnatural way. And do it six times in three minutes with three minutes rest and then do it again. Pat Cummins went into rehab for three years after one test. Imagine what a lifetime of bowling has done to the backs of the ubermensch who have carried the bowling load for CCC's Over 60s this week.

No wonder the rules of the tournament require eight bowlers to bowl. Imagine if captains had only to bowl six.

None of this is to be in any way critical of Canterbury's bowlers. Of course, CCC's bowlers now come from Mitcham and East Doncaster and the ranks of batsmen and the long retired. There is one or two home-grown CCC bowlers; but fewer than there used to be.

This is a long way of saying that CCC lost its second match today, with the bat ruling the ball. Our bowlers – our handsome, genuine, steely-eyed Keith Millers – were as diligent as you would expect. We just didn't have enough of them. And those we called on from the ranks of the batsmen and the long retired, as diligent as they also were, were – how can I put this – clearly from the ranks of the batsmen and the long retired.

So, we lost: 6/167 compared to VOSCA's 4/172, scored in 34 overs.

VOSCA put us in and Francis and Michael Loy, a real opening pair, took the score to 72 before the first and then the second wicket fell in the 15th over. Francis had scored a patient 36 while the next bat – what's his name again? – troubled the scorers not. We then had a mini collapse with wickets falling a 79 and 79 and then at 91. Our Mitcham import, Liam Peel was almost playing a full-blooded drive off the front foot when he was inexplicably given out LB. Redders, fresh from a forty, also succumbed to an LB. Steve Simpson, our other Mitcham import, played beautifully for 30, to help retrieve the position, before he too was LB'd. That was three LBs.

Finally, Bill Hansen and Charlie Morris came together for a combined score of 47, with Bill scoring a fine 36, his second-high score of the series. 6 for 167. About the same as Sunday's score but with a depleted bowling attack, a shorter boundary and a faster outfield.

Let's cut a long story short here…I'm getting tearful.

The first wicket fell at 79 in the 18th over, with Simmo taking a fine catch behind off a bottom edge. The next fell in the 22nd over at 112 as the injured Bill Hansen ripped out a middle stump. That was about it, really. The rest of the bowling attack tried hard; but I think we were up against it. They overtook us in the 34th over, which Peely bowled to three slips and a gully. Let's look at the bowling: Peel 0/28 off 8, with two maidens; Hansen 1 for 23 off 7; Morris 0/22 off six. All great efforts. The rest of the bowlers, batsmen all, couldn't match that performance.

Thanks to Liam and Steve from Mitcham and Redders from East Donny as well as Colin Peace who really did return from retirement.

We play our final game tomorrow.

Let's get up off the mat.

Destiny
CCC v Gold Coast

12 November, 2014
In his play, *Henry V*, Shakespeare creates a scene full of pathos, set on the evening before the battle of Agincourt.

Shakespeare has Harry make an impassioned speech to his closest lieutenants, his 'band of brothers'. In the speech, Harry inspires his men and – to quote the blurb for the recent Bell Shakespeare production of *Henry V* – 'confronts the fact that true courage and brotherhood can inspire remarkable achievements.' Bell's blurb writers assure us that 'this production will leave you feeling uplifted and exhilarated with the belief that the impossible is possible.'

Henry V contains an essential truth about how violence and conflict are often necessary as a threshold to triumph.

Is this intro to my report of today's match over the top do you think?

Yet the match was truly Shakespearean in character and plot, a game where the humble were made mighty, where the mighty were laid low and from which new heroes emerged, unexpectedly.

But to start. It was a surprise that this Agincourtian match took place at all. We only found out about the location this morning at 630am. Even Harry had more notice of where Agincourt was. But I bet he could never have found Narre Warren North.

The sides were evenly matched. Most of them were over 70 and they had nine. Most of CCC are not nearly 70 but, then again, there were only 8 of us. These were, nevertheless, better odds than Harry faced.

We had decided the rules of this particular battle beforehand. They were a bit like the Geneva Conventions in their complexity. We played 2 lots of 20 overs each. We changed no other rules.

Gold Coast – or the French, as we now fondly call them – batted first. After 20 overs, they were 2 for 75, with Billy Hansen and Charlie Morris having taken a wicket each. This seemed a reasonable score though our bowlers did have the upper hand.

We then batted and lost Francis at 22 in the fifth over. Our opening partnerships in this series have been 35, 31, 72 and 22, which have given us an edge in each match, some of which we squandered.

From there, the impact of our pre-match strategizing – our own Agincourt pathos – started to be felt. Michael Loy and Stockers proceeded to belt them all over the place with Michael retiring with the score at 95 (in the 15th over) and Stockers retiring when we were 99 (in the 16th).

The cricket gods then smiled on me and caused the French to bowl me many loose balls enabling me to reach 37 by our 20th over. At the 20 over break, we were 141.

Gold Coast doubled their score in the second half of their innings. But the game was played at a soporific pace and I had no cause to offer to swap my kingdom for a horse. The second half hero was Charlie Morris, who picked up 3 more wickets to finish with the magnificent figures of 4 for 16. All of you will know how rare a 4fa is. All bowlers performed well and Peely picked up another wicket. Remarkably, there were three LBs.

Rob Redmond and Peely resumed for us and after some Falstaffian efforts to bash the ball to the boundary, finally wiped off the 11 runs we needed to secure victory.

With no exaggeration, I think we can say the result, achieved with 'true courage and brotherhood', left us feeling 'uplifted and exhilarated'. The impossible may not be possible but we can beat a team of mostly 70-year olds.

Thanks to all who played this tournament, especially those without a prior connection to CCC and/or who played a very short notice – Charlie Morris, Andrew Day, Liam Peel, Rob Redmond, Jim Welsh and Michael Loy. Special congratulations to Michael Loy who scored 113 runs for the tournament.

I will, in due course, be providing a statistical supplement for the mathematically-minded.

By a Streat
Over 50As, CCC v West Ivanhoe, Hislop Park, North Balwyn

23 November, 2014

The Venerable Ones broke through for their first win of the season on Sunday, led from the front by David Streat and, in a reversal of trend, the ball wielded by Tex ruled the bat.

The Westies from Ivanhoe won the toss – another reversal of trend – and batted, as you do.

Theirs was a pretty solid effort, with four of the first five batters getting 20 plus. The bowlers suffered a bit in this season of batting supremacy with the quicks being eased to the boundary on a very fast running outfield. The slows fared a bit better, with Tex picking up three wickets and new boy Terry Hickey getting two.

Taking the pace off the ball looks like it's the captain's pick for this year.

I know there was some general grumpiness about the performance in the field but, hey, what about GG's outfield catch and his run out? And, here's a first, Laurie took a catch. Don't forget His Bobness caught one and stumped one.

OK, the general fielding may have to pick up; because fielding is the difference in this grade.

Anyway, WI got to 184 for 7, thanks to one late good innings, which Streaty ended with a perfectly timed catch.

I think 184 is about par at Hislop; that is, a competitive total which CCC would have to be on guard to match.

We did not start as well as we like with Bob out bowled in the first over to one that was too short to pull and to full to pull. So, naturally, Bob tried to pull it. Straight through for middle stump.

But the batting order is strong.

I had to leave early and didn't see the whole innings; but my imagination tells me it went something like this:

Mikey K played beautifully, working out how to hit fours when under leg stump attack from bowlers angling it across his body. His mid-wicket altercation with recalcitrant seagull did not disturb his concentration. 40 not.

GG was a little less aggressive than usual but played some tingling shots to the boundary for a fine 32. The nifty paddle shots he played to fine leg in the manner of AB de Villiers was the highlight of his innings.

Craig, playing his usual quirky and eccentric game, got a quick 26. I like to imagine 24 of those came in fours with two accidental singles. The fours would all have been from his favoured slapshot from balls that were identical but dispatched to different parts of the ground.

Roger played entertainingly for 2, all in singles, before he got out to the ball of the day – rising outside off after starting on leg – and the catch of the day, the keeper diving across two slips men to take the ball with his left hand coming back. No luck for Roger.

Streaty came in when the match was in the balance and drove and swept and pulled the team to victory. His running between wickets was a treat, despite two hamstring tears and a corked calf. 42 not out. Laurie chaired him off in a display of hero worship not seen since Laurie attempted to carry himself off in a display of hero worship.

Stockers, turning to left-handedness, played Chris Rogers to David's Warner and got a serviceable 20, including a well-run five.

The wise heads of Kent and Goldstein – is that a Saville Row gentlemen's outfitter? – calmly steered the ship home, albeit hesitatingly and with the usual panic well-disguised.

Canterbury 5 for 188 off 34.

David's post game text to me was suitably modest. But I think this was a pretty good win. And a great launching pad for the rest of the season.

Well done, boys.

The Cucumber Game
Over 50As, Mitcham v CCC, Mulluana Secondary College, Mitcham

18 January, 2015
Let me begin with a cliché. Some unkind persons will ask what is different about this match report.

Anyway, catches win matches. There, you have the story of the Legends victory over the top and undefeated team, Mitcham on Sunday at Mulluana College grounds.

Now, I don't wish myself to be unkind to the groundskeeper at Mulluana College. But the MCG it ain't.

Mulluana is the shape of a cucumber. 80 metres from the batting crease to six over the bowler's head. Nobody hit a six there. 80 metres wide. In total. 40 metres from the batting crease to the east or west boundary. Plenty of sixes were hit to both sides.

The general advice to fielders is: wear a mouthguard, to avoid the possibility of the ball hitting you in the mouth off a clump of the surface's uneven grass. I myself was a victim of the uneven surface, causing me – inexplicably – to let two boundaries through off Tex's bowling. Naturally, he was completely understanding and immediately forgiving.

And one more thing: the pitch was six feet wide. Do you know how hard it is to land a ball on a pitch that narrow? Ask Charlie, he had some experience of not landing the ball on the pitch. And he bowls straight.

Back to the game. We lost the toss; but to our surprise, we were invited to bat.

GG and His Bobness gave us a bright start. Bob was completely at home. Whether they bowled short or full, he just rocked back and pulled them past square for four and, on one occasion, six. Enough jokes about his penchant for pulling. It works for him. His quickfire 20-odd set the pace for the day. Regrettably, he chopped one on to his stumps, after the bowler realised that short balls outside leg are God's gift to Bob. Gary was more circumspect, Chris Rogers to Bob's Dave Warner. (Have I written that before?) Solid and comforting, that was Gary on Sunday. He ran himself out for a dirty dozen.

Mikey Kent was in superb touch, having had a full five minutes batting practice at Mulluana, his only batting since November. He played beautifully, placing – that's exactly the word – the Mitcham bowlers to all parts of the ground. His driving and lifted shots were a delight. If you only saw Mikey bat, you would not have believed how slow the ground was.

David Streat came in at four and he and Mikey were really pushing the score along. And it wasn't long before we were getting runs at 6 an over. Mikey eventually retired at 40 and I joined Dave. Clearly, the better bowlers came on at this point as the run rate slowed a little. Nevertheless, Dave and I added about 60 before Dave was bowled for 32.

Roger came and went quickly, I'm afraid; and then Charlie announced his presence at the crease with clean hitting and good running between wickets. His shot for six where he went with the momentum and just lifted the bowler gently into the school garden was memorable.

We were still moving along at six an over, taking advantage of the available singles with regular boundaries. I skied one to be out for 36 but Charlie and Goldy kept the score board ticking over. At the end, we were 5 for 206, with Charlie (38) and Goldy (8) both not out. A pretty good score but we hadn't forgotten that were we playing on a cucumber.

Early on, we saw why Mitcham had not lost a match. They are big, clean, aggressive hitters, who know their ground intimately. They are truly masters of the cucumber.

If we gave then width or balls short of a length, we knew where they were going: straight to the boundary.

But our bowling and catching were up to the task. Both openers were out by 23 and wickets fell so regularly they were 7 for 94 not long after drinks. Goldy and Tex had bowled a couple top-of-off but the day belonged to the fielders, at least to this point. There were five great catches: Roger at deep mid-on, Gary at deep mid-wicket, Mikey K at a deep and wide mid-on, Terry at a deepish gully and me at deep mid-wicket.

I think we relaxed a bit after the seventh wicket. But we won't do that again. Their last three wickets added nearly 100 as we forgot that they are masters of the cucumber and knew how to score quickly on their home vegie.

Eventually, Laurie came back and bowled their number 11 to give us victory by 15 runs. You always know when Loz gets a wicket. The world knows.

I think we all think our victory should have been by about 90 runs.

Bowling: Tex got four, which is a rare feat. It should have been five but I dropped a catch off him. Did I mention that? Laurie, Goldy and Charlie got 2 each. Deano was very unlucky not to snare a victim off his four overs.

So, we are third on the ladder, one point behind Ainslie Park and Mitcham, who play each other in the last game. If we defeat Warrandyte at home at CSG, we should finish second and get a home final. Let's not get ahead of ourselves; but we are well placed if we are good enough.

A Lot of Excitement Over 50As, CCC v Mont Albert Purple, Hislop Park, North Balwyn

8 February, 2015

Yesterday, someone said that the Over 50s was a bit like the Under 12s: a lot of excitement and not much skill.

Personally, I thought that was a bit unfair to both age groups – I've seen considerable skill in the Under 12s and, frankly, it would take quite a bit to excite some of those hard-bitten old guys.

Perhaps the first exciting moment of yesterday's game was when David Streat lost the toss (again) and Mont Albert put us in to bat. I'm sure that was excitement I saw on the faces of GG and His Bobness as they padded up.

The outfield was fast, very fast; Gary and Bob proceeded to hit the ball to all parts; well, anyway, they hit square of the wicket on the on-side. Theirs was a very entertaining partnership which totalled 11 fours and a six between them. Gary, who hit the six, wasn't sure he'd hit one since juniors. He was very complimentary towards the bowlers, who had put the ball exactly where he wanted. Now, I know we go on about Bob's pull shots but, seriously, he's very good at them. These days, he doesn't need a ball that short to see the opportunity for a four to leg. We should celebrate that skill.

Speaking of skill, Mikey Kent has bucket loads. He's having a marvellous season and got 42 not yesterday, including eight fours.

By the time first three had retired, I reckon the game was wrapped up.

The Older Kent and the Captain were together now. The Older was clearly playing for a 40 - and who would begrudge him that in his dotage. A slow start before he started to beat the bowling around the ground. He was dead unlucky to get out at 33. Some thought the catch had been taken as the fielder backed over the boundary line. Anyway, John is so good natured he walked.

David was out for 23 in curious fashion. He didn't think he hit it and neither did the keeper. But there was a loud appeal from most other fielders. Some things will always be a mystery.

Craig K played his usual style. I just love his straight drive from a cross batted slap shot. It's a delight to behold; and completely mesmerising for the fielding side. You can see then scratching their heads and asking: how did he do that?

I came and went, a testament to the 'lot of excitement and not much skill' aphorism.

Kurt was the recipient of the second curious episode of the day. Their keeper appealed for bowled off a ball that passed by the off stump; yet a bail had fallen. I was at the other end and he certainly wasn't bowled though the keeper honestly thought he was. I reckon Kurt's bat thumped on the ground, the vibration rattled the stumps and the bail dislodged. Any way, he wasn't out then. But was a short time later.

Charlie and Tex rounded off the innings.

We slowed a bit after the 21st over, scoring only 77 from the last 15 overs. But 239 is a pretty good score.

Mont Albert started well. But then the day's highlight: off a Billy Hansen outswinger, the batsman edged the ball which Goldy dived forward and to his right to pick up a brilliant catch centimetres from the ground at first slip. Tell me, how often do you see that in the 50s.

Four overs later, Goldy repeated the trick, though this time the ball came straight to him. Still, two slips catches off Bill's outswingers. Pretty exciting and lots of skill.

By the time the Alberts reached 60 in the 10th over, their second opener had retired and things ground to a halt. Over the next 11 overs we took four wickets for 29 and their last player (they only had 9) had a DNB next to his name. Two wickets to Charlie (off the first ball of each of his overs), one to Tex (bowled middle stump, cartwheel) and one to Terry H, caught Charlie, who apparently can catch. Not sure Streaty can. He dropped the same catch three times off Deano's bowling. True story. You gotta feel for Deano. His flight was excellent yesterday and he tempted the bats who were dropped twice more off his bowling. Still, Goldy's catching was a highlight and he is my official hero of the week.

Apparently, we are going to finish second, Eley Park having beaten Mitcham. Good news for us. Home final.

Now boys, let's hope we can see a bit less excitement and a bit more skill when next we meet.

Shock and Awe
Over 50As, CCC v Eley Park, Hislop Park, North Balwyn

22 February, 2015

George W Bush is credited and miscredited with many things. Proficiency at cricket is not one of them, though some people have a tendency to misunderestimate George.

Yet, I have wanted a way to work Dubbleya into a match report, an ambition I have now held for some time.

Well, here it: yesterday's result was shock and awe. Thanks, George. Mission accomplished.

Canterbury Legends had a convincing win over our old rivals, Eley Park in the Over 50s 'A' Division semi-final. I wouldn't usually point out what I am about to point out in the next paragraph, for fear of accusations of hubris. And regular readers of these match reports will know how much I loathe hubris, which always leads to a fall. But there are reasons for what I am about to do. Say no more.

Anyway, living dangerously, can I just say that Eley Park has not beaten Canterbury in the memory of any Over 50s player.

Hmm. Not sure memory is a good guide in the case of Over 50s players. But in this case, I think we can rely on our collective memory; some of it may still be intact.

The skipper won the toss and we batted. The Angley/Gavin combination made its usual attractive beginning, taking the score to over 30 – a useful start in anybody's language – before Bob and then Gary were both out caught. Here's the curious thing: both were out driving to mid-off, both seemed reluctant to play fully through the line of the shot they commenced with. I'm confident they'll both add new shots to their repertoires as a result of this experience.

Now the controversial bit. Mikey Kent came to the crease and, second ball, played the ball to short cover, following which there was a monstrous appeal for caught. Mikey stood his ground and the umpire ruled him not out: bump ball. Well, I can only speculate from afar about what the Parkers were saying about this but those used to lipreading Mitch Johnson will have some idea. The game was a bit spikey after this.

But Mikey was not spikey. He proceeded to score his sixth 40 not for the season, having now accumulated over 200 runs for once out. Keep it up, brother; one more time next week.

The skipper played his best innings of the season, 45 retired off 22 balls including three sixers and, obviously, one of them off the last ball he faced.

Another curiosity: Uncle John Kent also failed to follow through the line of his shot and was out caught at mid-off. Bad things come in threes.

Let's not dwell too much on the rest of the batters, except to say that they were very respectable in the circumstances they faced and, collectively, performed in a very team-like way. How else would we have got to 219, meeting Billy Hansen's requirement that we give the Parkers a tad more than a round number to chase. Apparently, if there is an odd number in your score, that is a psychological advantage to the side that batted first. I don't get it but I believe it.

Should mention Charlie Hall's 24 not out scored in the last couple of overs: we like that, Charlie.

So, after a somewhat frosty afternoon tea, we took the field. Now the Parkers are not a bad batting side and we were pleased to get out one of their openers for just 10, courtesy of a good catch by Bob off Billy's usual austere bowling.

The other opener was carving us up a bit but he was caught at deep mid-on. A fine catch, I'm told. Indeed, the catching all round was good. And Billy took his first catch in three seasons at CCC. Monkey gone, Bill.

Really, that was about the end of the story. After that, one batter got a paced forty but Tex (3/24) and Uncle John and Terry H (a wicket each) really slowed things down. Goldy, Billy and Charlie – why do bowlers always end in Y? – each also got a wicket. The bowlers were a bit like the German government negotiating with recalcitrant Greeks: give 'em nothing and ask 'em to repay it before they get it.

You can see the real affection in which I hold our bowlers, bestowing on them the praise I usually reserve for fiscal conservatism.

Our main challenge after the middle overs was to keep the pressure on, conscious of how we had let Mitcham off the hook when we had 'em down and out. We did and ended the game on a high note, running out Ziggy with a direct hit from the skipper. All out 164. Nemesis.

Yes, it was shock and awe. A 50-run win in a semi is a very good win.

And so to the Grand Final.

The skipper can expect a lot of advice this week. Here's my advice, skip: listen intently, make sure they know you love them and lead them to victory.

Tex's Hat
Over 50As, CCC v Mitcham, Hislop Park

Grand Final, 1 March, 2015
Hislop Park is deceptively pretty.

By which I could mean that it is not pretty but it deceives you into thinking it is. Or it is pretty when you don't expect it to be. I mean the latter.

From a distance, when your eyes perceive the outfield at an angle, the ground looks uniformly grass-covered; and smooth. The more so after rain, of which we had plenty on Saturday night. The surrounding trees have, over the years, added a certain middle-class suburban composure to an oval that was once a bit sparse.

Closer up, you can't avoid the bare patches in the grass, especially to the west; and you know that the ball will not always come at you with equanimity and grace.

I prefer to think about Hislop at a distance, from a narrow angle; with the trees as comforting backdrop.

It was against that backdrop, that David Streat won the toss in his first Grand Final as CCC's Over 50s skipper. V Mitcham. This was a big moment for Dave; and, I'd guess, one that contained a bit of apprehension; not that you'd notice. He's a cool customer, really.

The usual opening pairing took to the crease, a bit earlier than the scheduled one o'clock start. But, of course, we'd all been at Hislop early – Grand Finals do that to you. Oh, and did I mention the two umpires? We had two umpires; a real treat.

The match began in the familiar fashion with Bob scoring freely from the start. A good first over for us.

First ball, second over. Gary, LB. We would never had anticipated that. Was Dave suddenly under pressure, re-thinking the batting order and the game plan? Probably not. We bat deep.

Mikey Kent fronted up, five 40s on the trot, brimming with confidence, hamstrings loose, calves finely tuned. He began with suitable caution, playing in the V.

Nothing distracts Bob from his natural game and we wanted nothing to do so. Unfortunately, his natural game was interrupted quite soon when, at 14, he was out caught. 2 for 22. This is a rare event for us, two wickets so soon. And I think it brought a more sober assessment to our match day predictions, when the minimum bid was 200 and most of us were thinking 215.

Uncle John Kent once more joined his wide-eyed and expectant younger brother. From a distance, at a narrow angle, reading lips, I'm sure I saw Mike say 'What's the plan, bro?' and I'm just as sure I saw John say 'Play your natural game, boy.'

I have to confess, that when I looked at the scorebook to write this report, I was bit surprised to see John had amassed 25 runs. But he did. I put my surprise down to the fact that, at Hislop, runs have a welcome tendency to accumulate almost by themselves, with little or no help from batsmen. It's kind of mystical, really.

John's innings was a bit of a relief, taking us to 59 at the fall of his wicket. A relief because you can easily imagine – and my febrile imagination sometimes has this inclination – how 2 for 22 can turn into 5 for 40.

The skipper came in.

The next 7 or 8 overs did not take the uncertainty out of the game. After John's departure, the next three wickets added only 39, with Dave (11), Craig (5) and me (2) not playing up to our form. Ok, at least I played consistently with the natural batting gifts with which I was born.

I can't let Craig's innings pass without two comments: one, he looks like Darth Vader in his helmet and dark glasses and it's a pity the force wasn't with him; and they bowled nothing at him to which he could respond with his world-famous slapshot, the one he flats bats somewhere between point and straight hit, depending on his mood. I'm sorry he went as I love to watch him bat.

Liam Peel. Mitcham Captain and Honorary Cantabrian. Liam played for CCC in the Over 60s National Champs last year. So why did he feel that he could get three of our wickets? But he did.

Anyway, at 6 for 98 Roger joined Mike, whose hamstrings by now were no longer supple. Roge did exactly what he was supposed to do – belt them a bit and remind them that even at 6 for 98 CCC was not done for. Roger's departure for 14 with the score at 138 was the last time we lost a wicket.

Mikey retired at 40, having now accumulated 252 runs this season. Well done, Mike. The umpire, Gary, mistook me for Mike at one point; but I accepted his congratulations anyway.

We are blessed with batting depth. Charlie and Goldy proceeded to take the score to 179, Charlie scoring a brilliant 38 not out, well supported by Goldy with 11.

The thing about this final flourish is that Mitcham did not expect it. At 7 for 138, they must have thought we would be lucky to make 160. But Charlie and Goldy played with aplomb and skill. Honestly, I reckon this was the turning point of the game. Disappointed expectations are, I believe, a key source of subsequent under-performance. And, apart from our accomplished bowling attack, I think Mitcham's disappointment at not getting us out cheaply was one of the clues to our win.

During this time, I sat behind Tex and noticed, for the first time, the state of his hat which, I now realise, is a metaphor for Over 50s players everywhere.

Old, frayed, experienced, loved, not as effective as it once was, but serviceable enough to keep going without having to be replaced by a new version that might not see out even one summer.

When I knew Tex's hat was like that and that he kept wearing it, I just knew our bowling would be good enough to protect what was a competitive but by no means impregnable score.

We knew that one of Mitcham's openers had plundered Ainslie Park and set up Mitcham's semi-final win. We entered the field accordingly apprehensive.

The first over was uneventful. But the next two were pregnant with meaning. Both openers went, both caught behind by Bob. 2 for 9. Goldy and Bill had set up our victory. I learned later from Peely that these dismissals really hurt; not only on the scoreboard; but, I think, in Mitcham's collective mind.

Following these dismissals, Mitcham were under pressure throughout its innings. The psychological blow dealt by Bill and Goldy showed up in an over-abundance of caution that saw Mitcham falling further and further behind the run rate, conceding dot ball after dot ball and then having to find a four or better off the fifth or sixth balls of an over.

This is how it goes, as I said, when expectations are disappointed. Performance suffers.

Bill (1/16 off 6) and Goldy (1/23 off 5) set the scene for Tex (2/17) and Terry (2/22). Both bowled superbly, each getting two wickets and conceding only 39 off their combined 12 overs.

Mitcham's 2 for 9 became 4 for 48 and at drinks, they were only 63, compared to our 83. Mitcham's wickets fell regularly rather than in a rush (at 94, 121, 134 and at 155), when Deano – to the delight of all of us – picked up the final wicket to fall. Their respectable batting could not overcome the pressure of the increasing gap between runs required and balls left.

And they had to contend with some really good fielding. While we were occasional victims of Hislop's lack of equanimity and grace, we fielded very well. Only the most difficult of chances went to ground but the most difficult were also taken. Gary's catch on the boundary, running 20 metres and diving to his right were just sensational; and who can recall when a keeper last took 4 catches, as Bob did. Roger didn't put a foot wrong in the deep. I am even moved to compliment Laurie's fielding, though it's mostly done with his feet and not his hands.

We won. Actually, it was a relief. We've now won four of the last eight over 50s premierships but this one seemed to me to require something more challenging than the others. We were up to it. I think the best way to see this premiership is with quiet but deep satisfaction, acknowledging the best performances of our team mates but with a greater appreciation of the collective effort; and of the implicit understanding between us formed over many seasons together and which was the platform for this victory.

Well done, boys.

We Were Toast but We'll Rise Again

Over 50Cs CCC v North Box Hill Super Kings, Hislop Park, North Balwyn

October 2015

When you are making bread, the dough can sometimes take a little time to come together.

You measure out the flour, you add the yeast, a pinch of salt maybe, some honey or sugar and then you stir in the water.

For a while you may have a gluggy mess, in which case you add a bit more flour; or a somewhat dry concoction, in which case you add a bit more water.

Then you knead it a bit. Sometimes more than a bit.

Occasionally, it seems like the dough is never going to come together and all you have is flour and water stuck under your fingernails.

Creating a new cricket team is a bit like that. As the Over 50Cs discovered on Sunday.

Unexpectedly, I lost the toss and we were invited to field.

The North Box Hill Super Kings batted well from the start, keeping the run rate above four on an outfield that was running very fast.

We dropped a couple of early catches but we also took a number of early wickets and I thought we were on top even though they were scoring at four an over.

By drinks, the Super Kings were 4/83 and, I thought, were heading for a par score of about 180.

After drinks, the batsmen began to get on top. They played with controlled aggression and excellent running between wickets. They also batted deep into the order so that their number nine was very capable.

They had a couple of retirements before their innings ended at 7/207. They'd added 124 after drinks at nearly 7 an over.

Despite that, I'd say the bowling was pretty good. Mark Watkinson and Dean Galvin got two wickets a piece and new players, Peter Kemp and Michael Tiffin, each got one.

Roger Bryce took a bit of stick; but we all know that some days he can also break the back of an innings (and we expect him to do that at least several times during the season).

Neil Warner bowled his first over – serviceably – in 25 years; and Charlie Morris contained the batsmen during his two overs.

Our out fielding was good. And Gary Gavin took four catches behind the stumps, in an effort which looks like cementing him there for the season.

208 was a bit more than I expected to be chasing but is not beyond any team on a good day at Hislop.

We lost a couple of early wickets, Gary for 13 and Michael Loy for 3. Dean Galvin, opening the batting, played a solid innings of 38, including taking 12 off one over with three powerful boundaries.

The bowlers couldn't get Stuart out but he was having trouble laying the bat on the ball. Clearly, he was suffering a hangover from his Ashes Tour experience. The difference in pitch conditions was obviously on his mind. 40 retired.

We were in a bit of strife as the ask rose to 8 an over and then 10 an over.

I was lucky enough to face the less accomplished bowlers and got a quick 41 before Kurt and Neil Warner took us to 5 for 164 after our 36 overs.

We'd lost with a score a bit less than a Hislop par, 180.

Despite that, I wasn't disappointed and neither should you be.

The new team is a combination of a group of seasoned veterans who know each other well and a number of new players who have chosen Canterbury Cricket Club because of the quality of the cricket experience; or, at least, that's the reason I'm inventing.

We have all the right ingredients – a diverse and talented bowling attack, lots of batsmen and good fielding.

I expect the team to come together as the kneading continues into the second game.

The emphasis in this team is on participation, with everybody getting a chance to participate in all aspects of the game over the course of the season.

So, the blokes who didn't bat yesterday will be up the order next week. And those who were non-bowlers can expect to trundle down a few overs.

I think we can build a very competitive team on this basis.

Next week, the over-watered flat bread we produced yesterday will be replaced with a high top, floured, country grain Vienna, thickly sliced and spread with a good French butter.

A Mountain of Excuses Over 50Cs, Forest Hill v CCC, Forest Hill Reserve

25 October, 2015

What's the difference between a reason and an excuse?

The former seeks gainfully to explain while the latter seeks darkly to mitigate.

Frankly, I can't really see the difference.

By explaining, am I really trying to mitigate? Hmm. It's hard to know precisely one's own mind sometimes.

Perhaps it's better just directly to give a straight account of the facts; and successfully avoid the philosophical conundrum occasioned by the possible difference between explanation and mitigation.

So, what happened yesterday, when I think the Over 50s C Graders probably set a Canterbury Legends modern day record by regrettably losing our second match on the trot?

Well, first, I decidedly won the toss. And decided to bat. So far, so good.

Michael Loy and Neil Warner opened up. Neil was promoted in the order on account of his good showing last week with the bat.

Both were a little perplexed by that most ominous kind of bowler: the slow bowler who tantalisingly throws it up into the wind and gives the batter plenty of time to make four different decisions about where to hit it before finally settling on the big swipe, which the batter then misses and risks being stumped.

In Michael's case, it was more than a risk – he was stumped beautifully, for 2.

Neil suffered a different fate. Released from the slow bowler's perplexity, Neil felt so relieved to be facing the quick with the wind that he gave up his leg stump thankfully. Out for 6. But Neil has it still and I expect to see him among the runs soon.

By this time, Kurt Hansen and Michael Tiffin were together with Kurt playing well and aggressively. He retired on 42 with the score only 63 so you can see how creditably he was playing.

He is relishing the freedom to play that being near the top of the order usually endows.

Mark Watkinson joined Michael and played straight with accomplishment. Unfortunately, he was run out for 2. A run out is always inexplicable and so falls into the category of neither explanation not mitigation. It just is.

I joined Michael and enjoyed watching from the other end as he played beautifully all-round the wicket. He frequently makes good decisions about which balls to hit and where.

Retrospectively, I think we got on top of the bowlers with some good running between the wickets after we had sussed out which of the fielders had the slowest arms.

He retired at 40 after we had taken the score from 66 to 120 odd.

Compared to Michael, I was having trouble hitting the ball in the centre of the bat and was proceeding far more slowly than last week. And the boundaries seemed so much further away.

Our next four batsmen played manfully but not as accumulatively as they and we might have hoped. Brad Sheldon batted briefly but entertainingly for 4. Kurt's mates, our ring ins, Gerard Scalzo and Derek Djeng, got 9 between at the bottom of the order. Well done, boys, and thanks.

Did I mention that I ran Roger Bryce out? Thought not. Must have missed that. I was 37 no at the end, having batted an inordinately long time for that return.

At 6 for 161 we had finished competitively. But was it enough? Not as it turned out.

Their first three batsmen all got retiring scores and the first wicket fell at 137.

Not that our boys bowled poorly. Watto and Michael Tiffin bowled economically with the new ball. Watto conceded only 14 from his 4 overs. Michael bowled manfully considering the long spell he spent at the crease.

We (by which I mean I) thought that slower bowlers would spend the time more productively on a day like yesterday when we had to get them all out to win. So I persevered with Kurt, Roger and Brad for a lot of the day. They looked the most likely to get wickets even if they didn't.

If I'd had a slip, Brad would have certainly picked up a wicket or two. Roger did pick up a wicket with a ball that landed vertically on the leg sump of an unfortunate batsman.

Gerard Scalzo got the other wicket to fall with a Michael Loy nicely taking the catch behind. Which gives me the opportunity to compliment him on his keeping which, for a somewhat older gentleman, was remarkably agile and accomplished.

If he's up for it, he can keep the job indefinitely.

Anyway, they passed us after 27 overs which I think comes into the category of a 'good win' for them and a mountain of excuses for us.

What did we learn this week? There are four lessons:

We have a good batting team but we need to score more quickly at the start.

Ideally, we should be more attacking in the field.

Tactically, we need to be a bit more adventurous.

Preferably, I should use fewer adverbs when I write a match report.

Thanks to Dallas, Gerard and Derek, Kurt's footballing mates who played for us this week, ensuring we got a game. Thanks, boys. You're welcome back any time.

Disneyland
Over 50Cs, CCC v Mitcham, Hislop Park, North Balwyn

22 November, 2015

When they were little boys, Kurt Hansen and Derek Djeng played cricket in the backyard every day of the summer.

They'd rolled out a pitch, using an ancient roller they'd found abandoned at a defunct cricket club, in the bush, where they lived.

At first, they'd had to make a ball out of screwed up newspaper held together by sticky tape; and their bats were fence palings.

A couple of years on, they acquired some real equipment, given to them by the old lady next door, who'd got it from her son, a retired cricketer who been a district stalwart. The condition was that they not smash any more of her windows.

It was the seventies and Kurt and Derek emulated the stars of the time. Kurt wanted to be Dennis Lillee and Derek thought he bore a striking resemblance to Greg Chappell.

Both wanted to play for Australia and pictured themselves in a desperate last wicket partnership in which, against the odds, they snatched the Ashes from the reviled Poms.

Regrettably, neither Kurt nor Derek rose to the cricket heights they imagined as 12-year olds. But, on Sunday, they finally realised their ambition to snatch a last wicket victory from the gaping jaws of likely defeat.

I lost the toss to Mitcham's skipper and he elected to bat. Which is just as well as I had wanted to bowl first.

Our bowling looked a bit thin, with Michael Tiffin injured, Peter Kemp promoted and Watto struck down with illness.

But we had a plan: bowl full on or just outside off.

Brad Sheldon opened the bowling with me as his back up.

Mitcham's openers included Bennie, an old protagonist from the United Eagles. A terrific batter who had pounded us a few times in the past and did so again, for 40 not.

After six overs, Mitcham was 2 for 45. I had unexpectedly picked up 2 wickets though both Brad and I copped a bit of stick, obviously.

We, including me, put down a couple of catches which, I think, let them off the hook a bit. They had reached 104 for 2 by tea, with Bennie retired. A good score. Which looked like it could get a lot bigger.

But our bowlers stuck to it and stuck to the plan. All bowled well. Dean's five overs were testing for the batters and he was unlucky not to pick up a wicket. Roger is, in my humble view, always the bowler most likely to pick up a wicket, even when he doesn't. This time, however, he did. 2 for 17 off his five overs. Francis Bourke bowled very economically, 1 for 23 off 6. So too did Gary Gavin, 1/10 off 4 and Neil Warner, 1/7 off 3. We really slowed them down in the second half of the innings and they could only get to 162 after their great start.

Michael Loy took four catches behind the stumps. A great effort.

We started very well, with Gary Gavin in rare form, sweeping, driving and pulling. He was well supported by Michael Loy and the openers put on 42 before Michael went for 7, caught at forward square. He was quickly followed by Michael Tiffin for 2, same shot, same fielder, same result.

Mitcham's bowlers then got on top for a while with Deano, Roger and Bourkie struggling a bit against the slower bowlers. All three prefer the ball to come on to the bat but Mitcham's bowlers just couldn't bowl that fast. The highlight in this period of slow play was Roger's mighty six and Gary's retirement at 40.

At tea, we were 73; but still well in it.

Neil Warner was playing well, having regained his timing after a long period out of the game. Even at 5 for 88 (and with Gary retired) we still weren't out of it. Neil and I (21) took the score to 123. Neil followed at 128 (for 25) and Brad Sheldon (not many) at 129.

It looked a bit grim now. We required 34 off 42 balls and the last pair was in. Yes, it was Kurt and Derek.

The other twist to this story was that Derek had arrived to watch but was prevailed upon to suit up as we had only 10 players. He did this, emboldened by the two beers he'd already had and Roger's offer of fresh socks.

We were perched on the edge of our seats. No one was allowed to shift chairs. Only Michael Tiffin was authorised to change the scoreboard. Attestations of optimism were met with scowls and scepticism.

But we hadn't counted on the boyhood experience of Kurt and Derek; nor on the childhood bonding that makes heroes of ordinary men later in life. The spirit of that old lady from next door was surely watching down. (Am I over-playing this, do you think?)

Anyway, they proceeded to get the runs with intelligent and accomplished batting, mostly in singles. The rest of us sweated our way through it. The tension was real.

Derek (18no) hit the winning single off the second last ball and, for good measure, Kurt (19no) hit a four off the last.

Yes, it was cricket Disneyland; and dreams really do come true.

It was a great day. Perfect weather, a lot of fun and a game played in good spirit. The after match – when both Over 50s teams got together with their opponents – was a treat.

Well done, boys.

Sacrifice
Over 50Cs, North Balwyn v CCC, Macleay Park, North Balwyn

9 December, 2015

As I contemplate our loss last Sunday – possibly the worst loss I have experienced in Vets, apart from the time we couldn't make 88 to beat NBCC in a Grand Final many years ago – I turn to philosophy for comfort.

All sport, all exercise, involves a sacrifice. When we exercise or play sport, we give up something. Often, we give up something for someone else. For example, we might sacrifice our wicket in a wild swing in order to increase the run rate for our team.

Other times we give up something – like our afternoon – for which we might think there is no return. In a flogging such as the Over 50Cs just experienced, we gave up past glory for what seems like our immediate humiliation.

This sacrifice is not superficial mock-up.

Sport is a genuine arena of striving, pain and loss. It matters. And, of course, cricket matters most of all the sports. As JRR Tolkien opined in his essay, 'On Fairy Stories', 'The real enthusiast for cricket is in the enchanted state.'

But the enchanted state is no less worthwhile for being so. Jean-Paul Sartre wrote that 'the first principle of play is man himself' in which the aim is to 'attain himself as a certain being.' While we are never perfect, sport and its rituals are the means for us to grasp, for however short a time, the chance to possess ourselves and to be able to say 'I am this now'.

And yet, and yet…this enchanted state is only a secondary world. The sociologist Pierre Bourdieu calls this *illusio.* We do not give up reality for the secondary world.

We can return to the primary world, able to measure the sacrifice we made, to obtain satisfaction from it and to conclude that, at least for a moment, we had attained a certain being-ness. The result matters less.

Just as well. Because we really were flogged.

We batted first and our openers, Neil Warner (16) and Dean Galvin (10), dedicated themselves to what I think I can best describe as a very patient start. Their score was respectable enough though maybe a trifle slower than we hoped. But the bowling was tight on a turf wicket that helped the seamers.

We were under scoreboard pressure for most of the innings, with only Dave Crothers (18 – welcome back!) and Gary Gavin (12) of the remaining bats getting into double figures. We were all out for 98 in the 30th over.

Really, it was one of those days. Chris Hochen got three wickets. This was surely an *illusio.* What else do I need to say?

Then they batted. Our bowlers did attain a 'certain being' and I congratulate them for that. Unfortunately, their 'being' had nothing to do with cricket.

Suddenly, NBCC were 53 and one of their batsmen had just retired, enchanted. We continued to strive but experienced only pain and loss.

By the time I realised that Ronnie da Sliva (0/5 off 6) and Francis Bourke (0/7 off 3) were our best bowling bets, the game was over. They passed us in the 20th over.

And so we returned to the real world.

We made sacrifices, we were enchanted, we still lost. But we don't feel the sacrifice was wasted. We know that even the illusion of being-ness is worth it.

The secondary cricket world of our enchantment awaits January. We can manage until then.

BTW, Paul Grant made his return to cricket on Sunday, fielding. Next time, he'll bat and bowl if he wants to. Welcome back, Paul.

Dancing with Machiavelli Over 50Cs, CCC v North Box Hill Super Kings, Elgar Park, Box Hill North

17 January, 2016

In the sixteenth century, rulers and philosophers began to think and write about what we now call political science. Even though they thought about it, the rulers essentially were still inclined towards the Vladimir Putin school of politics: whatever it takes. Often enough, the 'whatever' was bloody violence of the anticipatory or retributory kind.

Nevertheless, they did think about what it would take to succeed in the murderous world of the sixteenth century, beyond the usual throat slitting, poisoning and garrotting.

Niccolo Machiavelli, one of my heroes, was among the first to think about the bigger questions of politics.

He conjured up two constructs that, he said, could help a prince succeed in achieving his aims.

One is *virtù*, the inherent, natural quality of the prince, a quality that the prince cannot change.

The second is *fortuna,* the luck and opportunity that is given to the prince.

The relationship between *fortuna* and *virtù* will explain the success or otherwise of the prince.

Without *fortuna, virtù* will not give the prince a way to gain the power. Without *virtù, fortuna* will be squandered.

A prince could be successful one day and ruined the next without any change in his nature. Two princes may use the same method, but only one succeeds. Two princes may use different methods, but reach the same goal.

You can see where I'm going with this, right?

Now, to the cricket.

Yesterday, CCC Over 50Cs fronted up the North Box Hill Super Kings, ladder leaders whose *virtù e fortuna* had clearly been well-aligned over the course of the season.

I thought deeply about strategy and tactics for this game; and late on Sunday morning finally ruled out on-field violence, to which I am less prone than I once was.

Instead, I focussed on cricket essentials: win the toss; front load the batting order so our better bats have the maximum chance to score the two or three 40s we would need to get a competitive score (the three 40s rule is, of course, the Bill Hansen rule, as you know); put bowling pressure on the Kings by bowling our most abstemious bowlers early; field brilliantly which, in our case, means drop fewer than three catches and put your knee behind the ball when fielding; appeal loud, confidently and long.

As you can see, my nature, my *virtù,* is now strategic, having seen off most of my cricketing *virtù*.

The 50Cs' collective *virtù* is in its cricketing talent which is, how shall I put this, differentially distributed but conscientiously applied.

So, with strategy, diverse skills and assiduousness our key *virtùs,* we were ready for the contest.

I lost the toss. But much to my surprise, we were put in.

We opened with Peter Haggar, playing his first game this year, and Michael Loy.

They started well, *fortuna* on their side; and they pushed the score to 25 before Michael was out for 10.

It was, at this early point, that despite our outstanding *virtùs*, *fortuna* began to desert us.

Michael Tiffin was run out without scoring. This hardly seems fair, let alone a reward for cricketing *virtù,* of which Michael has much.

Haggs and I continued, albeit in a sullen frame of mind; at least that was my mindset. Haggs was too exhausted to have a frame of mind.

Peter batted assiduously, overcoming the loss of his cricketing muscle memory, which he had not used for some time. His 40 retired was, as it happened, the only 40 we got. The Hansen rule did not even get a chance to be proved.

Kurt Hansen replaced Haggs, only to be caught at short point, again without scoring.

As you might imagine, this was a bit of a blow to our plans. But consistent with Machiavelli's thesis.

Francis and I got 20 and 21 respectively and the tail wagged, albeit in a somewhat desultory manner, less a wag than an occasional involuntary response. We finished at 9 for 131.

Of course, we rapidly did the re-calculations, based on a new-found knowledge of how the outfield was running: par was 160 not 180, a reasonable score was 140 not 160, so 131 was verging on a reasonable score, yes?

We opened the bowling with Charlie Morris and Francis Bourke, in a quest for spendthrift bowlers.

Apart from a couple of stray balls, they both delivered, Charlie 1/13 off 6 (of which 8 runs came off his first over) and Francis 1/22.

Haggs bowled tightly and frugally, but could only get in three overs before fitness and he had a robust discussion. He lost.

Following my own strategy, I appealed loud, confidently and long and got the correct decision for an LB plus a later bowled, 2/19 off six. Kurt picked up a wicket with his new style and Dean, as ever, bowled accurately and with guile outside the off.

I always bowl Roger when the batters have settled into a groove – on the grounds that batting grooves are a slow road to defeat for a bowling team and when Roger bowls, things happen. Roger, however, lacked *fortuna*. Machiavelli reminds us that it is only luck that changes, not nature. So, Roge, don't despair: your skill is still with you; but everybody has a bad day occasionally.

There were moments when we had a sniff, as they say. Only one of their blokes got a 40. But frankly, 131 is not enough when *fortuna* is against you. They passed us in the 31st over with a well-deserved win.

In consolation, I am obliged to recall one of Machiavelli's other constructs: sometimes, princes do not succeed because the circumstances do not suit their actions. Or, put another way, sometimes it all just goes to crap for reasons nobody will understand.

While we lost, we are not out of finals contention. The two teams below us both lost and remain a game in arrears. If we revive our *fortuna* to beat Forest Hill at home in a fortnight, we will be guaranteed a final and not have to rely on the *misfortuna* of others.

Nobody Told Me There'd Be Days Like These
Over 50Cs, Mitcham Yellow v CCC, Mullauna Secondary College, Mitcham

13 October, 2016
This won't take long.

Last Sunday, the Over 50Cs got flogged. By Mitcham Yellow.

On a cyclonic afternoon, at the ground least likely to host a game of cricket – a forlorn and abandoned secondary college – I lost the toss and CCC was invited to bat.

I'd have fielded too. Kurt's advice, good advice, was to field first – it would loosen us all up for the first game of the season. Pity I lost the toss. But would it have made any difference?

How do I put this? We were all out for 44 in the 20th over. Highlights? None to mention really. Roger, batting at 3, hit their opening bowler for six, which perturbed them for about a minute. Charlie Morris looked at ease for his 8 or 9 not out. The rest of us were nothing to mention.

They batted and despite the best efforts of our quicks (Brad Sheldon, 0/18 off six; Charlie Morris, 0/14 off six) and a good wicket by Mark Bellamy, volunteering from the Over 40s, Mitcham passed us in their 17th over. A big loss.

Paul Grant and Brian Clarke returned to cricket in this game. And it was pity we couldn't give them a better welcome back. Most peculiar.

A Perfect Day for Cricket Over 50Cs, CCC v Forest Hill, Hislop Park, North Balwyn

6 November, 2015
What a difference a month makes.

A month ago, on a cold, cyclonic day, on a dreadful ground somewhere in Mitcham, the Over 50Cs lost the toss and copped one Australia of a hiding. All out 44. Overtaken in the 20th over.

Fast forward to yesterday. The perfect cricket day on our synthetic home pitch. Which played beautifully, by the way; even bounce, the ball coming nicely on to the bat. A tribute to the pitch's curators.

The outfield was lightning fast, to coin a cliché.

We lost the toss and Forest Hill invited us to field. Thanks for that. We wanted to field, concluding that we needed to acclimatise ourselves again to the game of cricket.

Gerard Scalzo, who has a bit of nip, opened at one end, with Charlie Morris, who has more guile that nip, at the other.

Forest Hill's openers are a pretty handy couple. They play cautiously but punish the bad ball and run singles well.

We are used to our quicks being abstemious but the fast outfield put that expectation to the sword.

Nevertheless, I wasn't displeased with their efforts and was heartened when Charlie took out a leg stump with the score at 38 in the ninth over.

That wicket brought their best bat to the crease and he and the remaining opener pushed the score along steadily, though Clarkie is a different proposition altogether in C Grade and kept them under control. He was rewarded with a great C&B to remove the best bat. 2 for 84 at around about drinks.

Brad Sheldon took a bit of stick; but that happens a lot to faster bowlers on a good pitch with a quick outfield. We had to take the pace off the ball and who better to do so than Deano, who makes a virtue and a cricket career out of lack of pace.

They kept the score ticking over and their running between wickets was good. But they lost two wickets quick at 121 and 122. Michael Tiffin took a great catch off my bowling and then I caught their skipper for one off Deano. I know it looked like I was juggling an easy catch and made it look hard; but I deny that and Bob Angley's got the photos to prove it.

Over the next 30 runs, we took three wickets, two very good run outs (Morris/Galvin and Angwin/Galvin), proving that the slower you throw the ball the better your chances of a run out. Our run outs were not Temba Bavuma in action. Kurt got an LB: a full toss hitting the batter plumb in front.

Towards the end, they got away from us a bit and added 40 more to finish at 194.

I mentioned, just off-handedly, that 194 might be a very competitive score, using that euphemism to signal what I thought was the parlous state of our chances. Of course, in my own defence, I still had the Mitcham experience in mind.

But I was quickly disabused of my pessimism. Michael Tiffin almost hit a six in the first over, signalling back at me that they weren't bowling bullets and that, yes, CCC could bat.

Michael Loy departed for 5 with the score at 19 and Kurt left for 8 with the score at 57. Just dwell on that a moment: it shows how proudly in command Tiff was, eventually retiring at 41.

We didn't lose another wicket until we reached 175.

Deano 40 and Gerard 41 pummelled the bowling. Gerard had no need to run much, such was his boundary hitting. Deano usually has preference for boundaries when the circumstances permit. So, there was a lot of red in the scorebook from all the boundaries.

Still, by the time D&G had left, we still need about 50 in eight or nine overs.

I can't easily explain this but the ball just kept popping up at the right pace in the right place and we were able to hit it well enough.

Steve Watt, an unknown quantity, was playing his first game, batting at seven. His quantity wasn't unknown for long. He played just right for his 14, all of which came in boundaries. Work it out. That includes a big six.

I got some juicy deliveries from one of their mediums which allowed me to ping a few fours. That wasn't unusual. Everybody was doing it. We were making good progress.

Derek Djeng went for one, giving up the crease to Roger. By this point we needed 15 off three overs.

The ending was made for Roge. We needed 8 off the last two overs but Roge felt it needn't last that long. 4 and 6 to win the game then another 4 just to end any doubt. 19 not out, Roge. 22 not out me.

Our highest score since the Cs were founded and a very good win over an accomplished opponent. We won in a chase, which is both character forming and a boost to the spirit. A South Africa of a win.

The Hansen Exception
Over 50Cs, CCC v North Balwyn CC, Hislop Park, North Balwyn

12 November, 2017
Several years ago, when CCC had a team in the Over 60s national championships, I quipped that any team – in that case, us – with three players making 40 would win the game. As we walked off after our opponents had beaten us with four players making 40, young Billy added the Hansen Exception to my golden rule.

That was how our game against North Balwyn went on Sunday.

There was no toss. Long story. Ask me if you want to know it. The short story is that we bowled.

We opened with Charlie Morris and new boy Aarland Roth. Both bowled well but the batters were in very good form. We changed tack after 6 overs and Bourkie and Goldy took over. Yes, Goldy. He's back, all his mechanical parts well-oiled and tuned. You can barely notice the low-sheen glow of the electronics at work, especially through his whites.

But we couldn't make a breakthrough. I did drop a catch off Goldy, dislocating my finger in the process. I pulled it back together. Gosh, we're tough in the Cs.

One of NBCC's openers had already scored two 40s this summer and I was hopeful that his luck had run out. Sadly, I was disappointed. He proceeded to another 40 in a very good innings and left with the score at 79.

Their number three went first ball, caught by Johnny Papa off Bourkie, as he went to cut a ball that gently curled in the air to backward point.

Perhaps our luck had changed. No, it hadn't. Their second opener got 40 and they didn't lose another wicket until the score was 155, when Charlie, with a throw to Michael Loy at the stumps, ran one out. Our bowlers, Deano, Watto, Marky Mark (love the new wheels!) and John, had slowed them down. We picked up two injuries, a hammy (John) and a calf (Brad).

They belted us a bit in the last six overs with two more 40s. 2 for 196 at tea.

To be frank, I wasn't optimistic, especially after I asked Brad and John to run a bit. They couldn't. So, duty of care and all that, I took them out of the batting order.

Michael Loy and Goldy began slowly and with deliberation. Gold was out for 13 with the score at 26 and Deano went in.

This was a slow point for us, and at one stage, there were 15 or 16 dot balls in a row. At drinks, we were just 45 and things looked a bit challenging.

We picked up the pace after drinks with Michael getting to 40no in a very patient innings. Teams always need an opener who can hang around. Dean's timing had asserted itself by now and he, too, had picked up the pace.

I was getting the benefit of a few half volleys and some short ones going down leg and put a few away before I ran Deano out for 35. Derek joined me and looked in good touch before falling to what I think is one of the greatest catches I've ever seen. No exaggeration. A hoick to deep mid-wicket, the sweeper runs to his right, dives, takes a one-hander just off the ground. I clapped. It was a ripper. And not real bad for someone over 50; or at any age for that matter.

Really, with two overs to go, it was over too. I hit a four off the last ball to get to 40. But we were well beaten.

It's hard to think what we might have done differently. Two catches dropped. Well, it happens. Otherwise, the fielding was good. Our bowling wasn't bad even though it suffered a bit at the end. I could have bowled Johnny Papa a bit more and me a bit less. The initial batting was a bit contained but the bowling wasn't bad either. The bright news is that we scored 100 after drinks, which is good in anybody's game. Michael Loy's innings was a great strength for us and I thought Mark W was looking good with both bat and ball. Derek fielded exceptionally well. The main thing, I think, is to think through what we do when the batters are hitting us around.

Anyway, we back up next week. John and Brad…keep that ice on your lower extremities and don't take any risks.

The Consolations of Philosophy
Over 50Cs, Forest Hill v CCC, Forest Hill Reserve

19 November, 2017

This morning, I spent some time searching my bookshelves for Alain de Botton's darkly idiosyncratic *The Consolations of Philosophy*. Because God knows, I needed some consolation after yesterday. (Note to self: I probably shouldn't bring God into it when I'm being philosophical.)

de Botton has chapters on consolation for frustration, inadequacy, unpopularity and difficulties. I needed all of those chapters to reflect on the Over 50Cs' performance and even scanned the ones on a broken heart and not having enough money. Surely something would ease my pain.

You might have guessed that we lost yesterday.

My state of mind was such that, in my post-match speech, I speculated that we had never been so outplayed when we fielded as we had been by Forest Hill.

The day did not begin as I would have wished when I lost the toss and we were invited to bat when I had wanted to bowl. The first frustration of the day.

Nevertheless, we decided to make the best of it, as Seneca, the Roman stoic, would have wanted us to do.

And we did pretty well. The openers, Francis and Kurt, were steady and well, prolific would be too strong a word, but productive kind of captures it.

They put on 52 before the first wicket fell (Francis, 22), several overs short of drinks. This was, in fact, a very reasonable effort and did not warrant any of the feelings that provide de Botton with his chapter headings. Though I suspect Francis' heart is always broken when he is dismissed.

Then followed the time-honoured middle order collapse. Johnny Papatheohari went first ball, Charlie Morris missed a full toss and was bowled for 1 and Steve Watt kindly took a step back and positioned his legs immediately in front of the stumps, promoting me to give him out for a duck. I detected feelings of inadequacy in the middle order.

Boys, please see chapter IV in *Consolations;* or go to the source, Michel de Montaigne, whose recipe for dealing with inadequacy is to think that life as a goat is much preferable to life as a human.

We were suddenly 4/61 and in 'difficulties'. Nietzsche, one of my favourites, gives good advice about 'difficulties': welcome difficulties in the search for fulfilment. Who wants to abolish suffering anyway? What a man!

Kurt and Aarland Roth are clearly fans of Nietzsche too as they proceeded to restore order before Kurt was out for 34 with the score at 78.

Aarland kept searching for fulfilment, getting to 23 before getting out with our score at 98. Lou Berigman came and went for 6 with his sunny disposition at odds with the difficulties we still faced. I'm sure he's read all of Montaigne's work; and I'll have to talk to him about life as a goat.

Derek Djeng and I then put on 40 as we upped the pace a bit, bolstered by de Botton's observation that fulfilment is reached by responding wisely to difficulties, which I did before an unwise attempt to hoick the slow bowler over his head saw me stumped. Derek was soon run out for 28, having played a very good knock in the best stoic tradition, before Goldy notched up 5 at the end.

156, including 100 after drinks. With 5 scores of 20 or more. Not a bad effort but I'd have liked 20 more. Captains always want 20 more, just for adequacy's sake.

Charlie and Aarland opened our bowling and were quite economical though without luck in their opening spells. The first wicket fell at 50 when FH's skipper tickled one to Michael Loy behind the stumps off Goldy, who had bowled well too. If only I could field him in slips off his own bowling.

A second wicket fell 12 runs later when I C&B'd the other opener. FH was ahead of the pace by this time and starting to get on top of our bowling.

All of the reasons why we needed consolation became manifest during the next few overs: frustration, inadequacy, difficulties and broken hearts as no bowling change seemed to work and the ball was constantly played to the position I'd just shifted a fielder from. Personally, I find it very frustrating when a batter with no skill or elegance whatsoever somehow belts good balls, pitched on a length over the bowler's head off the back foot. How does that work?

Aarland finally got a well-deserved LB decision and they were 3/125 but there were still too many overs to go.

John Papa bowled 6 respectable overs and will be better for it. And I'll be bowling Lou earlier and more often in future.

They passed us in the 31st over, with a four off me over mid-on.

Good bits? 100 after drinks, 5 scores of 20 or more, Derek's and Kurt's good form with the bat, a good opening bowling pair in Morris and Roth, John P's progress as a bowler, Francis's fielding and fielding overall. Bad bits? Sorry, room for improvement: a few more runs before drinks and keeping the ball pitched up and off the leg stump.

Facing one's difficulties, struggling with them and maybe even overcoming them, is the key to finding fulfilment. In cricket too. I'm sure that somewhere, sometime, Montaigne wrote something like that.

Sympathy for the Old Enemy
Over 50Cs, CCC v Deakin CC, Hislop Park, North Balwyn

20 December, 2017

I know how Joe Root must feel. Cook is cooked, Vince is minced and Joe, well, he's not himself, is he?

Nothing he does can stop the rot. Good batting doesn't get him over the line. A plan only survives long enough to be replaced by another plan.

That was our day last Sunday.

We lost the toss and were invited to bat by an opposing skipper who looked and sounded pretty confident. I didn't quite understand the reason for my unease at the time; but I knew something was up.

Actually, in the circumstances, we did pretty well prior to drinks, even though the total contribution Lou and I made to the score was less than one. Kurt and Roger (welcome back!) made modest contributions but Goldy and Barry King (also welcome back!) both got 20-odd, which took us to 5 for 60 at drinks.

I admit, this did not look that great. But the best was yet to come.

After drinks, we had our best batting session of the year. Derek Djeng batted brilliantly for 42 not out, hitting them to all parts of the ground. One or two aspects of his technique might need a bit of polishing but there is no doubt about his hand-eye coordination.

Johnny Papa came from nowhere to knock up 25 no, slamming fours and sixers everywhere to push our score up to 172 in the last couple of overs. Dean (14), Charlie Morris (9 no) and Aarland (4) lent DD and JP good support.

I've learned to be more hopeful than confident in this position. We had a plan: bowl full and wide of the off stump, make 'em drive and hope for some catches. I could not have anticipated what came next.

I knew the writing was on the wall when their opener hit Charlie's second ball back over his head for six, the ball bouncing off the top of the drinks container and disappearing off somewhere into suburbia. This guy retired before the end of the fifth over. I had frightening visions of our nemesis, Elbow, the first time we encountered him, hitting Gary Gavin out of the ground in much the same way. But better.

I tried my other plan: take the pace off the ball. That always works. No, it doesn't.

It didn't get any better though I tried hard to convince the team that things had returned to normal after the opener departed.

In a sense they did. Two more batters got 40 no, Goldy picked up a couple of wickets, Dean got one and Charlie got the LB he deserved during his second spell.

But, really, they were playing with us.

I tried some intimidating field placing. Silly point. Another four behind square. That spot Jimmy Anderson fields in when Steve Smith is batting. Four through covers.

Nothing worked. Nil. Nix. Nought.

They passed us in the 28th over.

We congratulated them and slunk off as unobtrusively and humbly as possible to the BBQ. Outclassed. Thank Heaven for hot snags and a cold beer.

Have a great Christmas.

Victory at Last
Over 50Cs, Yarra Junction v CCC, Yarra Junction Reserve

21 January, 2018

Prelude. One of the most important insights I acquired in a long career in industrial relations is that unions always claim victory, whatever the circumstances.

I have seen unions claim victory when they've had to break up a strike they were on the verge of losing, when a court case goes against for them, when one of my clients manufactures a clear media advantage out of nothing.

The great strength of unionism is that union officials are brilliant at turning a defeat into a strategic and tightly held myth that sustains them for decades and decades and binds their members to them.

As a result, one of the most critical pieces of advice I give my clients, who are rarely trade unions, is to claim victory as often as possible; and to do it early and often, before unions do.

The match report. Yesterday, in the superb surrounds of Yarra Junction Reserve, tall eucalypts in the foreground, purple hills in the background, the Over 50 Cs scored a stunning victory over Yarra Valley.

The win began when I won the toss and decided to bowl. My rationale was that I would like to keep Yarra Valley in the game as long as possible and to give my bowlers a good spell to sharpen their skills for the final game of the season.

My judgement was spot on. Our openers, Charlie Morris and Johnny Papa, had the Yarra boys tied up in knots for over after over. The consequence was that I had to take them both off, Johnny after three and Charlie after four, in order to keep the Yarra in the game.

The Yarra had to eke out the runs, one at a time, painfully.

We picked up a couple of early wickets to have the Yarra in deep trouble at two wickets down with hardly any runs on the board.

Deano replaced Johnny and, in a superb tactical move, forced the Yarra's captain to hit him into the vacant space I had created between mid-on and deep mid-wicket. Wily as ever, Dean kept bowling to the captain's strength, allowing him the false confidence to think that he had our measure. The handful of fours he hit really showed how on top we were.

Lou bowled four overs of extreme line and length and with Goldy at the other end, swinging them out and cutting them in, the Yarra's bats didn't know what hit them. Or where to hit them.

I could only challenge them with a couple of overs from Roge and one over from Steve Watt before I came on myself to make sure we bowled out our full complement of 36 overs and maximised our bowling trial.

Michael Tiffin, back from injury, bowled six of the last 12 overs, along with Charlie and Lou, in their second spells.

Stumps knocked out of the ground by your quick is one of the finest sights in cricket and we were lucky enough to see Charlie do it twice.

Wickets keep falling regularly as we moved inexorably to our first clean sweep in two seasons. We got the Yarra all out!

The Yarra interrupted this joyful occasion with an excellent afternoon tea and a warm message of welcome.

Then, our batting was a purist's delight as we carefully navigated excellent bowling from the Yarra.

Nobody would dissent from the view that theirs is one of the most accomplished and frightening bowling attacks that has ever been seen in Over 50s cricket anywhere. It is a tribute to our batters that they played the bowling with such aplomb and flair.

Tiffin batted patiently as he sought to re-accustom himself to competitive cricket and, in the end, went for 39, dancing down the wicket to their quickest bowler, only to be caught at long on in a brilliant catch that saved a six.

Michael Loy, our Joe Root, withstood all they could throw at him, before succumbing as he doubled the scoring rate that had heretofore been the norm.

Goldy was swashbuckling in his energy. Never before have I seen anyone buckle his swash in such a threatening manner.

Roge went in at four, his role well-defined. He was to bamboozle them with his aggression and lack of orthodoxy. This proved so successful that no one knew he was out bowled. He and Tiff had run at least three before someone noticed Roge's off bail had mysteriously displaced itself. Roge, ever the sportsman, offered to walk and left to loud applause.

Barry came to wicket and stepped up the pace as I joined him in a run frenzy, highlighted by a two we ran to a ball I played back to the bowler. I was out to the ball of the day. Someone measured it a 144 kph and another swore that it swung in a least a metre from outside off stump. It surprised even me that I was still able drive it in the air nearly to the cover boundary before I fell to a remarkable catch, the fielder sprawled to his right taking a spectacular one-hander.

After Barry's departure and after Steve had unselfishly sacrificed his wicket for the team, Francis and Johnny Papa delighted in sharing an unbroken partnership that took us through to stumps.

Here is the measure of our victory:

1. We got them all out
2. Only one of their batters got a 40
3. Charlie's two bowleds were spectacular
4. Goldy continued to impress with a well-thought out and economical spell
5. Lou has proven himself a very useful bowler who will benefit from his long spells

6. Roger is on the mend and will be a terror for Warrandyte in the final round
7. Welcome back, Tiff. A great 39
8. Francis is having a Second Coming
9. Johnny Papa can both bat and bowl
10. I can take a catch, eventually.

So, a victory all round and at last.

Post-script.

Aloha
I may be wrong but, technically, wasn't that a loss?
Bewildered.
Waikoloa, Hawaii
Sent from my iPhone
Laurie Cavill

Aloha
What, just because they outscored us? That's a very narrow way of seeing the world.
Surrey Hills, Victoria
Sent from my iPhone
Michael Angwin

An Escapade in the Country Over 60s, Warrandyte CC v CCC, Warrandyte Reserve

21 October, 2018
Well, Warrandyte is hardly the country. But for those of us who seldom go east of Union Road in Surrey Hills, it's quite a trip.

And an escapade too. Which, as you all know, involves excitement, daring and adventure.

Charlie Hall can attest how being captain, which he was today, brings one into contact with all three.

First, Charlie won the toss and, in an act of daring, decided to bat.

Michaels Angwin and Loy opened up against some tight bowling which proved a bit too exciting for both of us. Michael the Elder was bowled by an in swinger in the third over – for four. Michael the Younger stuck around for a while as Kent the Younger embarked on his own adventure. But the remaining Michael was out in over number 8 for 7.

Things didn't improve. Craig went for 17 with the score at 36. Our captain, new bat in hand, hardly had a chance to use it before being caught for a duck and Deano, injured, was run out for 1. We were 5 for 50 and the excitement, daring and adventure had given way to something that resembled a looming defeat. (Note to aspiring writers: never, *never* say looming defeat. Say any kind of defeat – unanticipated, unexpected, overwhelming, even crushing. But never looming).

At this point, the crease was occupied by Broc, John Hine, our country recruit. And by Goldy.

Broc is a broccoli farmer. For those of you who have had a long day, 'Broc' is a diminutive of broccoli. (President George HW Bush once said: 'I don't have to eat broccoli. I'm the President.' You can imagine what happened next: the broccoli farmers of America sought an audience in the Oval Office where HW was fed his broccoli by his wife Barbara and professed his unending love for the green sprouted vegetable of the brassica species. Rest assured Broc, all your team mates eat broccoli for breakfast, lunch and dinner. Except Bill.)

What an adventure this partnership turned into. The next wicket didn't fall until the score reached 108, giving us a chance at a competitive total. Apart from Goldy's perfectly timed cuts and his hoick (technical batting term) over square, the highlight was his straight drive – straight, that is, back at Broc who took it square on his thigh, just above where the cow had kicked him on Thursday morning. Life's a real adventure down Bairnsdale way.

Despite both bruises, Broc put together a well-made 33 and impressed with his pull shot, albeit one played with less compulsion and with less frequency than Bob Angley's. (Inside joke.)

Anyway, 'Dougie' Walters didn't stay for long, LBW for 5. Going back to a straight ball pitched full can sometimes result in that unfortunate outcome.

Goldy then retired at 40, his second maximum for the season.

We were 6 for 121 at this stage and still defeat loomed. But JAK and Peter Kemp played adventurously and with daring, exciting the large crowd into a ululating fervour. I'm kidding. The large crowd barely ululated.

By the time they had finished with Warrandyte's bowling, we had reached 7 for 171, maxing out at 179 as the innings ended with Bill Hansen at the crease. Now, defeat no longer loomed. As the skipper said, it wasn't an above par score. But it was defendable.

And defend it we did.

The Dyters made a good start, taking fours off our opening bowlers, Bill Hansen and Charlie Morris, with apparent ease in the first couple of overs as they quickly raced to 25. Mid-way through his third over, Charlie struck, Goldy diving to his left at slip to take a ripper of a catch. Goldy said of his catch that, sometimes, the cricket instinct takes over even though the mind knows that following the cricket instinct can only result in pain. We have these insightful, nay philosophic, exchanges from time to time in the 60s. We've got plenty of time to think.

In his next over, Charlie struck again, with Bill taking the catch. I was expecting to see pain but Bill had too long to think about it.

John Kent was living up to his own expectations with, first, one wicket and, second, another wicket, with exciting catches to Craig and to Deano, who once again failed to drop a catch, keeping his perfect catching record intact. By this stage, WCC was 4 for 42 and the game had switched from looming defeat to possible victory. I knew this because the team was smiling again. Smiling usually accompanies success as frowns accompany looming defeats.

We kept the pressure on them after this through abstemious bowling. Kemp (0/14 off 8) and Angwin (0/12 off 5) bowled without generosity. One of WCC's bats got a 40 and was part of a partnership that took them from 42 to 87. But WCC was struggling to get the rate up to the necessary four and a half.

Their captain played a well-judged innings of 24 before, adventurously, he took off for a cheeky single only to realise that JAK can throw the stumps down from 20 metres despite what people say about him.

JAK and Broc gave up a few runs but by the early 30s overs it looked like we were heading to victory.

Hansen and Morris came back at the death, neither giving much away and Charlie picked up his third wicket for 24. WCC 6 for 142. Canterbury Over 60s had its first and historic victory, an exciting, daring and adventurous win if ever there was one.

What did we learn? Four things:

1. We may have been a bit cocky coming into the Over 60s but we are competitive nevertheless.
2. Fielding can make a real difference. We caught and fielded well all day while WCC dropped four catches in two overs at one stage
3. Our talent is deep and wide: we can recover because of it.
4. Both our opponents in the first two games have gone out of their way to welcome us warmly and have emphasised the spirit in which cricket is played by old fellas. I think we are fully aligned with that.

Our next game is 18 November. Feel free to play Over 50s until then.

Well done, Charlie, on being a winning skipper and on the quality of your leadership.

Caledonian Sunset Over 60s, Iona v CCC, Iona Cricket Oval

13 January, 2019
Iona is a small island off the west coast of Scotland.

It is known principally for two attributes: the many contentions about its real name and the Iona Abbey, a symbol of Scottish monasticism for three centuries – until the monks sensibly abandoned their celibate and humble ways.

There is no dispute that Iona Cricket Club's actual and historical name is 'Iona Cricket Club', though some thought it bore a resemblance to The Poplars*, minus the pub, the boundary hedge and the gentle climate. In other words, Iona CC's rustic ground and infrastructure bore no resemblance to The Poplars at all. And, despite the blustery easterly that made any form of conversation impossible; and the fact that Iona CC is about as isolated as its namesake island off the west coast of Scotland, we came away with a kind of affectionate respect for the tin shed in which we escaped the wind and the somewhat narrow pitch on which we played ourselves to eventual victory.

Because our players left celibacy behind eons ago and because they have rarely been humble, I have no excuse to chase any further the many literary opportunities provided by the once thriving nature of Ionian monastic life.

One of the theories about the derivation of 'Iona' is that it means 'man of yew'. As you know, 'yew' is a tree of considerable longevity and resilience, which seems appropriate in light of the fact that Deano captained us on this occasion. In future, when we address him as 'Hey, Yew', there will be no mistaking this sign of respect for the less complimentary 'Hey, you' – even though he lost the toss and we had to field.

We underestimated Iona. Their batting was better than capable and the results entered on My Cricket this season do them no justice.

Billy got our first wicket early with one of the best C&B's you will ever see, diving to his left to pick up a chance that Dwayne Bravo has dropped many times. I had a clear view of this – Billy's hand was a bucket from which no ball would have escaped.

Charlie Morris wasn't so fortunate. Despite his usual reliable line and length, he had 15 taken off one over as ICC's bats proceeded to flay us a bit. There was on LB of Charlie's which was surely out, though the ump's eyes must have been blinded by the Ionian sun.

They also flayed me. Is 50 off eight overs some kind of record? Anyway, I finally got a wicket in my 8th over and then a second as two wickets fell with the score at 113. This was the 25th or so over and Iona was making its bid for victory.

While I apparently bowled pies from the southern end, Goldy had a much better record into the wind, 8 overs, 1/17; and ICC was 4/114.

This setback at 114 was temporary. Iona didn't lose another wicket as they managed player participation by retiring four batters. Deano tried a few bowlers – himself, Bourkie, Broc and Dougie – but without really making a monk's curse of difference to the scoring rate. At over #34, Iona was 164 and 200 seemed possible. Deano then recalled Billy and Charlie who stopped the bleeding and finished off with three maidens in a row.

ICC, 4/176 (cc). A pretty good score though we thought par was 200, having revised that down from 250 as the outfield was slower than it looked.

We felt pretty confident that we'd get the runs. Once again, we underestimated Iona.

Our openers were sensational, pounding Iona's bowlers all over. Pup, as Barry King has come to be known, belted them for 14 in one over on his way to 41; with Michael Loy almost as voluptuous in his scoring rate, before being stumped for 22.

Goldy and I were now at the crease as we proceeded to prove the theory of the 'hollow middle'. This is my theory, my attempt to bring intellectual respectability to the reasons why the early middle order quickly hollowed out 1/62, turning it into 3/83. The Hollow Middle is no longer a theory; it now has an accepted place in cricket life, on par with the Hansen Exception as an explanation of the course of a cricket match.

It's simple, really: after a great start, you can always count on the middle order to fail and bring some drama to a game that looked won after 7 overs. Goldy and I did this by getting out for 9 and 2 respectively.

The impact of a Hollow Middle is to place greater pressure on the Lower Middle. But I must say that Deano (9), Dougie(11), Kevie (5) and Charlie (2) withstood it well, scoring modest but valuable runs as we entered that part of a game of cricket where the match really is in the balance and stays that way for the rest of the innings.

We lost our 7th wicket (8th with Pup's retirement) at 140, with Francis still in and Broc now with him. We needed 37 to win with two wickets in hand. Plenty of overs but we were still rightly worried.

This was the best innings I've seen from Francis. Calm, measured and in control, complemented beautifully by Broc's characteristic heterodoxy. Francis and Broc kept the runs ticking over, taking advantage of extras and with the occasional four to relieve the pressure.

I was sitting with Bill, who was showing signs of wanting and not wanting to go out there and smash CCC to a win.

In the end, he could take the pads off, as relieved as an Ionian monk ordered but then excused from physically chastising himself for eating the extra tuber that was really the Abbott's.

Francis and Broc got us home at the end of the 36th over, with two wickets intact. So, really, we smashed them, didn't we?

Deano, who last captained a side 50 years ago – with a victory then – kept his winning streak going.

The wind did not abate, even as the sun began to drop below the lone tree that provided shade for all of west Gippsland's dairy herds. Silently, we drove off into the Caledonian sunset, victorious once more.

(* The Poplars is a cricket club in Gloucestershire UK, where CCC's touring party played an enchanting 20/20 game one mellow Friday evening in 2018.)

Not Seen in the Cricket Pages of Major Newspapers Over 60s, CCC v Koo Wee Rup , Hislop Park, North Balwyn

17 February, 2019

The sandpaper scandal provided Australia's cricket journalists with a year's worth of stuff to write about.

One of cricket's biggest stories was Warnie's ingestion of a diet pill to smooth his forehead wrinkles.

Why the Punjabi Wobblers paid a fortune for Ben Stokes makes headlines.

Who can forget Hansie Cronje's corruption?

And what about the fight between Simon Katich and Michael Clarke?

Or Gat's hi-jinks?

Without human weakness, cricket journalists would have nothing to write about. They excel in human weakness and have learned how to write about it without getting sued. But they still know too little about cricket.

Without scandal, corruption, money and sex, the cricket pages of our main newspapers would only be filled with boring things like someone making a century or a duck or getting five for or getting that hat trick or taking that catch behind square. Oh, and they'd have to write about who won and maybe why the won.

You won't find any of the salacious, sleazy interesting stuff in these CCC match reports. No way, dude!

And you won't get over-produced analysis of the opening over or the drive to point or that really complex stuff about 'technique' (of which there is very little anyway in our game).

What you'll get here is a summary of the scores and who won, a bit about the flow of the game and a conclusion about why the result was what it was. I learned how to do this in year 9.

Summary of game: Canterbury Over 60s 5/213 defeated Koo Wee Rup Over 60s 7/134. *Result announcement*: Canterbury won.

Match description: Skipper M Loy won the toss and we batted. JA Kent was out third ball caught at square. M Angwin hit a couple of good fours before playing the worst shot of the season to be caught at slip for 12 (*self-deprecating humour*), 2/37. A Goldstein made 40 not out including two watchable sixes off their best bowler. Then, three wickets fell quickly at 94 (K Cullinan for 1), 95 (J Segar, first ball duck) and 96 (C Hall for 27). Two of these were LBs given by B Hansen. We noted that Hansen is a bowler whose LB appeals are often rejected.

Flow of the game comment: CCC looked a bit vulnerable at this point but there was plenty of batting to come. At drinks we were 5/100.

Those three wickets in the mid-90s were the last wickets to fall. FW Bourke, determination on show (*expert comment*), retired at 37. P Kemp made 43 not out with a multiple of shots to many parts of the ground (*observation skill on display*). The skipper made a lively (*adjective used for colour*) 18 not out with B King coming in for the last over, as we sat glued to our seats in anticipation; and hitting three fours! (*Sentence construction used to create tension).*

CCC 5/213.

Lunch time summary: a competitive score on a ground with a rapid outfield, possibly a par score in the day's conditions.

Koo Wee Rup presented two very capable openers (*condescending compliment)* who scored freely against the C Morris/C Hall opening attack. One them was felled by a rising ball and retired, returning later to be felled again by a rising ball and retiring again (t*oo obvious an attempt at humour*). J Segar and J A Kent replaced the Charlies and – *flow of game comment* – stopped the free flow of runs with 12 overs that gave up only 21 runs with two wickets to J Segar. *Another flow of game, expert comment*: one wicket was a bowled that cut back 15 centimetres and the second was low down catch at slip by A Goldstein.

M Angwin bowled four overs for one wicket, stumped by B King and was, he claimed (*affected comment to introduce controversy*), deprived of a second stumping by an umpiring error.

A Goldstein and P Kemp (2/17 off 4 overs) closed out the game which (*insightful observation)* had run out of much interest.

Expert analysis: On the day, CCC was the better side. The batting had depth, which meant that the low scores that some contributed were balanced by the high scores by others. CCC also has many capable bowlers. KWR had three excellent batters and a couple of very good bowlers but, on balance, did not have CCC's depth of talent. CCC's fielding was good and superior to KWR's, which let through many fours that CCC did not.

Philosophical conclusion: A very good win but not one that should give rise to complacency. We have seen too often how good wins morph into subsequent bad losses when hubris (*elitist word requiring dictionary*) arrives.

A Dance to the Music of Time Over 60s, CCC v Australian Cricket Society, Jubilee Park No. 2, Frankston

24 February, 2019

'A dance to the music of time' is both a 17th century painting by Nicholas Poussin and a novel in twelve parts by Anthony Powell. The painting is regarded well but the novel is one of the finest of the 20th century.

Powell takes the painting as the inspiration for his often-comic examination of movements and manners, power and passivity in English political, cultural and military life in the mid-20th century. The story is narrated by its leading character in the form of his reminiscences. This is an irresistible source for an Over 60s match report. I shall humbly take the role of narrator.

First the painting: four figures, holding each other by the hand, dance in a circle, as Time plays a lyre on the right.

There is no doubt who Time, the lyre-player, is. It is Francis Bourke, to whose tune we all danced yesterday, stopping every several moments so he could adjust the choreography (and the field) to suit his take on the game. I can assure you that, unlike the lyre-player, Francis does not play naked though the wings are entirely appropriate.

The scene is set in the early morning, which accurately reflects the time we left our homes to travel to Jubilee Park in

Frankston, where we played the Australian Cricket Society on turf. Beautiful ground. An Elysian Field.

The procession in the sky is led by Aurora, or Charlie Morris, the goddess of dawn, which is about the time Charlie picked me up. We travelled to Frankston in what seemed like the chariot of Apollo. Actually, we needed a chariot to lump all the cricket gear and match day infrastructure we needed for a home game we played away.

Apollo is the sun-god in the sky behind Aurora. But I did not sit in the back.

You're probably asking yourself: what does that ring represent? I'm guessing but I'd say that it is probably the Zodiac, a recurring theme in 17th century classical art portraying the essentially random trail of life. Does that sound like I just made it up? It looks like a wicketkeeper holding the ring. Poussin's cricket genius is yet to be recognised.

In the distance, you can just catch sight of a cricket ground which, of course, was a common sight in both Italy and France in the 17th century and provided inspiration for many a painter. Can you see the turf pitch and the sight boards?

The four dancers, beginning with the one at the back seen mostly from behind are Poverty (Craig Kent and Dean Galvin, whose batting return was far from rich), Labour (reflecting the way we went about our batting and bowling yesterday), Riches (of which we had some: Morris 25, Segar 27no, Angwin 24no; but not enough), and Pleasure (of which we had none, at least in the result).

These figures represent a progression in human life, completed by Pleasure leading to Poverty again – which I think is the way ACS's skipper, Stuart Stockdale, summed up the game. They were on top, we were on, they were on top until, at the end, we returned to the Poverty of our second loss of the season. We can, however, be heartened by Poussin's symbolic return to Pleasure once more, perhaps at the Echuca Carnival.

The two cherubs on each side of the dancers are clearly Kev Cullinan and 'Dougie' Walters, our recruits this season. They are still the babes of our team and Francis was right to note that their completion of innings in which they batted together and in which neither was dismissed was a sign of their presence. Next season, however, they will both be wrinkled and naked, new lyre-players both. My only question is: what are they holding? Is that Kev smoking and if so what; and is Dougie drinking a beer?

Frankly, I'm fascinated by the two-faced stony figure on the left. I think it was Goldy's bowling. It is a long time since he was dealt with in the way Stockers fixed him – and us – up yesterday. The far-left face was Goldy as he started his spell and the near-left after he finished: older and wearied.

Movements and manners, power and passivity, the core platforms of Powell's story, explain yesterday's game and much about Over 60s cricket.

Movements. Sometimes there are none. Them in the field and us in the field. At other times, the game was marked by superb running between wickets, both us and them. CCC Vets, Legends and over 60s has been marked by quite defensive fields, which encourages our opponents to take those quick (relative term) singles. Francis tackled this serial error yesterday, with closer-to-the-wicket field placings. I think was can learn from this. Speaking of movement, Roger ran a two.

Manners. Oh, how mannered is over 60s cricket! We are so polite. We clap our opponents and we are nice to umpires. Dissatisfaction with an umpiring decision is muffled words and hand gestures withheld. A fielding move requiring little more than a bend of knee attracts rapturous applause and verbal praise – 'oh, great fielding; was that Mark Waugh I just saw'. After match speeches are full of praise for the teams that you have just flogged and whose batting and bowling you have just plundered. Example: Stockers was so nice to us after our flogging yesterday. Even one's opponents take time to mention the fact that your drive off their bowling through cover was a delightful shot played off their best ball. We had to concede yesterday that manners had nothing to do with our loss. We'd have been beaten even if we'd had Dave Warner's on-field sensitivity.

Rules, I think, come under the heading of manners. Yesterday, we played according to the rules to apply in the Echuca over 60s Carnival. The main innovation is that batters must retire after 30 balls. This reminded me of the party scene in Part 3 of ADTTMOT, at Mrs Andriadis's place in Hill Street in Mayfair. Suffice to say here that the relations and the conversation and the action at the party were conducted according to highly structured norms and rules which, in the end, resulted in some surprising outcomes, some unexpected relationships and some sober lessons learned. Before you reflect on the lessons we should learn, you'll have to read the book.

Power. Can I say it again, Stockers' innings was the difference. What we lack in physical power these days, we make up for with....with....hmm, I'm not sure.

Passivity. This seem like a low note to end on. So, I won't mention it but perhaps it segues into the scores: CCC 8/156 defeated by ACS 5/158.

End of the first season for the Over 60s. Well done, boys: six wins, a tie and two losses. Let's reflect on the season and share our reflections.

The Palace of Wisdom
CCC at the Echuca Over 60s Club Championships

March 2019
William Blake, in *Proverbs of Hell,* tells us that 'The road of excess leads to the palace of wisdom. The tigers of wrath are wiser than the horses of instruction.'

Blake's theory, which gives rise to his proverb, is that progress in life is impossible without 'contraries', the opposing forces within us all – excess and wisdom; emotion and instruction.

Mounting the horses of instruction, we planned our assault on the Echuca Over 60s club championships. We agonised over our batting and bowling orders and fielding technique; and strategized ourselves to death in figuring out the best approach to the 30-ball rule. (For the uninformed, that requires a batsman to retire after facing 30 balls but entitles him to return after all other batsmen; except if (1) he scored 40+ off his first 30 balls or (2) if 10 wickets have fallen, which might have happened because we were able to bat 12). On field, we workshopped what to do next when things were going badly.

The planning helped a bit. But, yes, the tigers of wrath are smarter than them dumb horses. We learned a lot more from the tiger of our crushing defeat than we gained from the horse of our cold, clear planning. The pain of uncontrollable defeat is a wiser teacher than all the instruction that any horse can give you.

As it happens, I am sometimes told in my private life that the clarity of my logic is a lot less admirable and compelling than the emotions that I should be allowing to surface more often. I think that amounts to 'go tiges'. I'll take more heed of that from now on.

You are probably wondering about which 'road of excess' we were on and how it led to the 'palace of wisdom'.

I confess that there were several roads of excess we all travelled which had nothing to do with cricket; but we did not let the dinners, BBQs and pub nights slow us down. The 'road of excess' whose navigation leads to the wise palace is the four games we played in five days. That's a lot and by day four all of us slowed down. And our defeat by new rivals, Sunbury, was also a push and shove in the direction of wisdom.

By the end, we were wiser men. Wiser about bow to manage our bodies and wiser about how to play the game. I'm not claiming we are not permanent residents of the palace; but, hey, all that pain must be worth something.

Game 1: CCC v Endeavour Hills, Victoria Park, Echuca

We won the toss and batted on a slow pitch with a slower outfield.

The tigers were ascendant as we proceeded to lose 3 for 15, Roger Bryce, Michael Loy and Barry King departing cheaply. Goldy (32 in two stints at the crease courtesy of the 30-ball rule) and JAK (20no) brought stability back to the innings, helping take the score to 65 before Peter Kemp (9) departed on an early horse. John Segar and I were now at the crease and kept the score ticking over with lots of singles, as the tigers chased us down the pitch. I was out off my 30th ball (18) with the score at 100 before we had another mini-collapse (Craig 2, Charlie Morris 4, Kev Cullinan 2 and Broc-a-duck). Goldy returned to the crease but another tiger gobbled him up and we were out for 128 in the 38th over.

This did not look good and clashed markedly with the vision I had had of our performance pre-game and before I had read the *Proverbs of Hell*, into which I now feared we had descended. Our only excuse was that the pitch was very slow and the outfield slower. Endeavour Hills did well, with their opener, who also opens the bowling for Over 70s Australia, doing particularly well (2/11 off 5).

As it turned out, the tigers whose wrath Endeavour Hills encountered were much hungrier than the ones that we faced. We were convinced John Segar had an LB first ball but it was turned down. Despite that, our bowling was on top. We were anxious for most of the innings because 128 is not easy to defend. But, in two spells each, Goldy 5/5 off six – the best bowling figures of the tournament – and Segs 1/3 off five tells you most of what you need to know. Kempy, JAK and I got the other four wickets. It was tense at the end but that makes for a very satisfying victory. Our fielding was good and that helped a lot.

We prepared for the next day's game by going to the official meet and greet at the Moama Bowling Club, off which we are all now members.

Game 2: CCC v Sunbury, Bamawn Lockington United CC, Bamawm

Here's a picture of me losing the toss and, with it, the match.

This was a flogging. They had four batsmen who faced 30-balls and reached a retirement score. One of them got 40 off his 30 balls while their lower order Juggernaut scored 53 off 25 balls. The 30-ball rule permits that. We were still in it when the score was 4/171 off 35 overs but The Juggernaut effectively ended the game. We felt the hot breathe of tigers for most of the morning on a good wicket with a fast outfield. Sunbury 6/216 off 40 overs.

Good news? We ran out 4 of their batsmen, proving that we can still accidentally hit the stumps with a random throw.

Enough of that. Bamawm is about 35 kilometres south of Echuca and you get there by driving through bare, brown country which is the last place you expect to find a cricket ground that is actually green. But it was. Bamawn's history and present state are the counter to big cat wrath. What strength and commitment must there be in a rural community to produce such a ground. In the clubrooms, you can see

Bamawn in its earlier incarnations: the old tennis club, the superseded cricket clubs of Bamawn and Lockington; and the now-defunct footy club. Frankly, these memories give me more warmth than what I am about to tell you about our innings.

At 0/49 off 10 overs, hope and optimism had – for a while at least – replaced the negative psychology that cricket teams sometimes go through when they think they might just be playing a team that is better than they are. The Kents got 23 each and Barry K got 22. But the lives of hope and optimism were nasty, short and brutish. The highest score among the next nine batsmen was 7. We were all out for 100 after 31 overs. Their best bowling figures were 4/10 and 3/6.

We were rapidly reinventing our ambitions for this tournament as, now, we couldn't be division winners.

What a difference a day makes. Goldy went from 5/5 to 0/35. And The Juggernaut made a duck in Sunbury's next game. Cricket's a cruel game, yes?

Sunbury clearly feels an evolving rivalry with CCC, perhaps because we demolished them in our contest during the season. In my after-match speech, I reminded them that they had now only drawn level with us at 1 each.

John and Lyn Kent invited the team for a BBQ at their caravan park and we turned the ignominy of defeat into a celebration of charred meat, healthy salads (the traditional Kent coleslaw was prominent) and their usual alcoholic accompaniments, of which we, of course, drank moderately in anticipation of the next day's rest.

Game 3: CCC v Warrandyte, Windridge Oval, Rochester

Thank heavens for the rest day. Without it, we'd not have been able to get back on the pitch. We had no specific injuries but our bodies were speaking their age.

Windridge Oval, named after the late local champion Bill Windridge, is a magnificent facility, built with the best that flood relief can provide. The old oval was flooded out in 2013 and the new rooms are the result. The pitch and ground were superb and some of us shed tears at the comparison with Hislop Park. The feature I liked most is the wide verandah and viewing area, which is complete with overhead fans to soothe one's sweaty brow after a brilliant innings or bowling performance. The pitch was a ripper. The sad thing is that the ground is now rarely used for cricket. But I'm prepared to volunteer CCC Over 60s for a match there most weeks. Rochester also has one of the most spectacular country pubs at which you can drink too much at after the game. Not that we did that.

Here's us at the Bowling Club. We didn't have a drink all night.

I returned to toss-winning form and we batted. Kempy and then Goldy went cheaply and we were 2/23 but the rest of the batting was among our best of the tournament. We had 5 retired: Loy 15, Broc 23, Angwin 22, Segar 27 and C Kent 16. Barry King got 28, out for the second time off his 30th ball. JAK played a brilliant innings of 24 at the death. After the compulsory closure, we were 5/188. The running between wickets was a feature of our game in this match.

Warrandyte's batting was slow against the good bowling of Segar and Morris, now both injured (glute and knee respectively); and Kempy. Goldy (knee) was also indisposed and he didn't bowl. We got their best bat out cheaply and their first three batsmen got only 16 between them. One of them retired for 7 after his 30 balls. We loosened up a bit at this stage and more of our bowlers got an opportunity to test their talents. Again, the fielding was good with a couple of run outs the highlight. Their middle order had some success – three retirements totalling 64. But we bought the higher order bowlers back and Warrandyte were 6/133 after the 40 overs. Kempy got two and Segs and JAK one each.

A good win. No tigers were displaying wrath and the horses were again in command.

Back to The Bowling Club for the official dinner and the news that we would be playing one of the tournament's franchise teams, the Rolling Stones, at Bunnaloo, about 45minutes drive to the north of Echuca.

Game 4: CCC v The Rolling Stones, Bunnaloo

Another drive into the country, through brown fields with the occasional sheep or cow.

I added to my toss-winning streak by winning a second in a row and we batted again. How country cricket clubs produce such wonderful grounds and pitches in what is, for us, the middle-of-nowhere, is a continuing surprise and delight. Is cricket strong? You bet.

If Game 3 was among our best batting performances, the batting in this game was the best. Six batsmen retired after 30 balls: Kemp (22), Goldstein (13), King at last (25), Morris (28), C Kent (19) and Deano (21). In addition, JAK got 27 in another superior end-of-innings performance. You've finally found your spot, John; but please find some new pads. At the closure, we were 5/183 but fivefa only because Segs and Broc threw away their wickets in the run chase.

The Stones, an Over 60s franchise team, batted well and their talent was evenly spread. While we were always going to win the game, we did have to re-focus during the last 10 overs to ensure our victory. Yesterday's injuries were mostly under control though all of us were feeling the effect of a week's intense cricket.

We turned to Goldy for six overs just to put the skids under the Rollers and rein in the scoring rate. He repaid our faith with 3/14 off six. Other wicket takers were Morris, JAK, Segar, Kemp and Angwin. The Stones, with a spike right across their backs, were all out for 156, giving us a comfortable win.

The highlight of Bunnaloo was the hospitality – the best since T3. What a wonderful lunch the ladies of Bunnaloo put on for us. I was particularly delighted with the jelly slice, which I haven't seen since I was a child. It was magnificent.

The Wrap

All in all, we finished third in Division 2's eight-team, dual-dual conference competition, one spot behind the grand finalists. A good start but our rise to Division 1 has been delayed a year. We need to get the balance between tiger and horse right. We've had enough excess to drive us closer to the palace of wisdom. The rest we'll do on our own. A couple more players would help to spread the load over 4 days of cricket. A left-arm orthodox slow bowler would be a great addition. Does anybody know a 60-year-old leg spinner?

And let me commend the swimming pool at the Paddlewheel Motel for after-match recovery.

Post-script

Blake knew a lot about cricket.

In his cricket poem, *The Echoing Green,* he foretold our experience in Echuca this week:

...our sports have an end:
Round the laps of their mothers,
Many sisters and brothers,
Like birds in their nest,
Are ready for rest;
And sport no more seen,
On the darkening Green.

That's us: ready for rest. Oh, believe me, I am ready for rest.

CPSIA information can be obtained
at www.ICGtesting.com
Printed in the USA
BVHW091418160221
600262BV00021B/1109